The Min

Wales

NEVER YORK • LONDON • DELHI

NEW YORK • LONDON • DELHI

www.roughguides.com

Credits

Author (Rough Guides): Matthew Teller
Editor (Rough Guides): John Fisher
Editorial (Visit Wales): Annmarie Graham and Geraint Thomas
Editorial Coordinator: Emma Traynor
Layout: Link Hall
Cover design: Diana Jarvis
Cartography: Edward Wright
Proofreader: Diane Margolis

Adapted from The Rough Guide to Wales by Mike Parker and Paul Whitfield, with additional material from Visit Wales.

Project managed by Remote World Ltd (DOD)

Published by Rough Guides Ltd,
80 Strand, London WC2R 0RL

Photography © Crown Copyright 2007
– Visit Wales Image Centre

Front cover image: Llangennith, Gower Peninsula
Welsh Language image: Rhossili, Gower Peninsula
Back cover image: Porth Dinllaen, Llŷn Peninsula

Contents

Introduction

Perched on the rocky fringe of western Europe, **Wales** often gets short shrift in comparison to its Celtic cousins of Ireland and Scotland. Neither so internationally renowned nor so romantically perceived, the country is usually defined – if it is known at all – by its male voice choirs and tightly packed pit villages. But there's far more to the place than the hackneyed stereotypes, and at its best, Wales is the most beguiling part of the British Isles. Even its comparative anonymity serves it well: instead of being reduced to some misty Celtic pastiche, Wales remains brittle and brutal enough to be real, and diverse enough to remain endlessly interesting.

Only 160 miles from north to south and 50 miles from east to west, Wales still manages to pack in a huge variety of stunning, wild landscapes, magnificent beaches and fascinating history. Its **mountain ranges**, ragged **coastline**, lush **valleys** and old-fashioned **market towns** all invite long and repeated visits. The culture, too, is compelling, whether in its Welsh- or English-language manifestations, its Celtic or its industrial traditions, its ancient cornerstones of belief or its contemporary chutzpah.

Recent years have seen a huge upsurge in Welsh self-confidence, through music and film as well as the arrival of a **National Assembly**, the first all-Wales tier of government for six hundred years. The ancient symbol of the country, *y ddraig goch*, the **red dragon**, seen fluttering on flags everywhere in Wales, is waking from what seems like a very long slumber.

With its rocky and mountainous landscape, sparse rural population and a culture deeply rooted in folklore and legend, Wales shares many of the hallmarks of its Celtic sisters, Scotland, Ireland, Cornwall and Brittany. To the visitor, it is perhaps the **Welsh language**, the strongest survivor of the Celtic tongues and one of Europe's oldest living languages, which most obviously marks out the country. Tongue-twisting village names and long, bilingual signposts point to a glorious tale of endurance against the odds, slap next to the heartland of English language and culture. Everyone in Wales speaks English, but a quarter of the population also speaks Welsh: TV and radio stations broadcast in it, all children learn it at school and visitors are encouraged to try speaking at least a fragment of its rich, earthy tones.

Although it's often the older aspects of Welsh and Celtic culture, from **stone circles** to crumbling **castles**, that initially attract visitors, contemporary Wales is also a draw. The cities and university towns throughout the country are buzzing with an understated youthful confidence and sense of cultural optimism, while a generation or two of so-called "New Age" migrants have brought a curious **cosmopolitanism** to the small market towns of Mid-Wales and the west.

Perhaps most importantly of all, Welsh culture is underpinned by an iconoclastic democracy that contrasts starkly with the establishment-obsessed divisions of England, or even, to some extent, of Scotland or Ireland. Wales is not, and never has been, so absorbed by matters of class and status as its near neighbours. Instead, the Welsh character is famously endowed with a **musicality**, lyricism, introspection and sentimentality that produces far better bards and singers than it does lords and masters. Anything from a singsong in the pub to the grandiose theatricality of an *eisteddfod* involves everyone – including any visitor eager to learn and join in.

Getting around

The cities and densely populated valleys of South Wales support plenty of **train** and **bus** routes, linked in with the British national network, but the more thinly inhabited areas of Mid- and North Wales are less well served. Of course, with a **car** – your own or a rental car (easily picked up in most towns and cities) – you'll be able to see a lot more of the country in your own time.

The most reliable source of comprehensive, impartial information on public transport throughout Wales is **Traveline Cymru** (☎0871/200 2233 ⓦwww.traveline-cymru.org.uk).

By train

Two main lines provide frequent, fast **trains**: from London Paddington (via Reading and Bristol) to Newport, Cardiff and Swansea; and from London Euston (via Crewe and Chester) to Llandudno, Bangor and Holyhead. Connections at Cardiff or Swansea link up with onward services to Carmarthen, Pembroke and Fishguard, while slow, picturesque railways trundle through Mid-Wales – to Aberystwyth, Pwllheli and the "Heart of Wales" line through Llandrindod Wells – from Birmingham or Shrewsbury.

You can **buy rail tickets** at stations, from major travel agents or online at ⓦwww.thetrainline.com.

Train information

Arriva Trains Wales ☎0870/900 0773, ⓦwww.arrivatrainswales.co.uk. Principal operator for most of Wales's rail routes, with timetables and ticket sales online.

First Great Western ☎0845/700 0125, ⓦwww.firstgreatwestern.co.uk. Timetables and tickets for trains to South Wales (Newport, Cardiff and Swansea) from London Paddington, Reading and Bristol.
Great Little Trains of Wales ⓦwww.greatlittletrainsofwales.co.uk.

Grouping of nine narrow-gauge steam lines, with various discount deals.
National Rail Enquiries ☎0845/ 748 4950, ⓦ www.nationalrail. co.uk. Timetables, fare details, comprehensive rail maps and up-to-date information on track problems and engineering works for all train services throughout the UK.
Virgin Trains ☎0845/722 2333, ⓦ www.virgintrains.com. Timetables and tickets for trains to North Wales (Llandudno, Bangor and Holyhead) from London Euston, to Cardiff from London Paddington and from around the UK via Crewe, plus some trains to Newport and Cardiff from Bristol.

By bus

Inter-town **bus** services duplicate a few of the major rail routes, with fares often substantially lower than the train. The biggest operator is **National Express**, which has many services from English and Scottish cities to Cardiff, Swansea and West Wales as well as to Wrexham and the North Wales coast.

Within Wales, you'll often be relying on **buses**, which provide a much deeper penetration into the countryside than the trains. They are run by a bewildering array of companies, though timetables and routes are generally well integrated, even if some far-flung spots are a little poorly served.

Bus information

Arrivabus Cymru ⓦ www.arrivabus .co.uk. Major bus operator for North Wales and the Cambrian Coast.
Bws Caerdydd ⓦ www.cardiffbus.com. Bus operator in and around Cardiff.
First Cymru ⓦ www.firstcymru.co.uk. Runs many bus services in Southwest Wales.

National Express ☎0870/580 8080, ⓦ www.nationalexpress.com. Long-distance bus services throughout the UK.
Royal Mail Postbuses ⓦ www .postbus.royalmail.com. Network of picturesque postbus routes – carrying mail and passengers – linking isolated communities in the rural backcountry.

Tours

Although you may want to see Wales at your own speed, don't dismiss the idea of booking your trip via a **tour operator**. Some of the backpacker tour operators listed below run regular bus services throughout Wales allowing ticket holders to get on and off at each overnight stopping point and rejoin the tour when the next bus (or the one after that) pulls through. These are particularly suitable if you're on a budget and fancy travelling with like-minded individuals. You can stay where you want, though most people book into the YHAs and independent hostels recommended by the tour company. More conventional operators offer slightly more upmarket bus tours, including meals and accommodation; these take the hassle out of getting around the sights, and can often work out cheaper than accommodation and transport booked independently.

Tour companies

Anderson Tours ☎ 0870/1111 400, ⓦ www.andersontours.co.uk. Trips by luxury coach from London to Cardiff, Caerleon and Caerphilly Castle.

Back Roads Touring Co Ltd ☎ 020/8566 5312, ⓦ www.backroadstouring.co.uk. Leisurely-paced escorted minibus tours for 1–12 people to discover "the real Wales", travelling via back roads.

Bicycle Beano Cycling Holidays ☎ 01982/560471, ⓦ www.bicycle-beano.co.uk. Sociable 7-day cycling holidays (July & Aug) in Snowdonia and the Pembrokeshire Coast National Parks, fuelled by delicious vegetarian (and mostly organic) meals.

Bushwakkers ☎ 01874/636552, ⓦ www.bushwakkers.co.uk. Trips themed around canoeing in the River Wye or pony trekking in the Brecon Beacons National Park. Meals and accommodation included.

Discovery Wales ☎ 029/2066 6879 or 07849/067449. Provides expert guides for walking, hiking, cycling and coach tours, ideal for independent travellers. All guides are qualified to degree level and are officially accredited Blue Badge guides for Wales.

Dragon Backpacker Tours
ℸ01874/658124 or 07977/148295,
ⓦwww.dragonbackpackertours.co.uk.
Flexible, small-group tours led by
expert guides. Private and packaged
options available.
Explore Wales ℸ07899/012578,
ⓦwww.explorewalesnow.co.uk.
All-inclusive tours that take in the
landscapes and culture of Wales.
GTS Tours ℸ01843/293399,
ⓦwww.gtstours.co.uk. Weekend tours
combining the North Wales coast with
the magnificent mountain scenery of
Snowdonia National Park.
Haggis Adventures ℸ0131/557
9393, ⓦwww.haggisadventures.com.
Award-winning adventure tours for
independent travellers, including a
3-day "Welsh Dragon" tour with local
guides and a 7-day Britain trip visiting
Wales, all departing from London.
Karibuni ℸ01202/661865, ⓦwww
.karibuni.co.uk. Multi-activity
adventure weekends in Pembrokeshire
and Snowdonia National Parks,
including horse riding, mountain
biking, surfing and hiking.
Road Trip Tours ℸ0845/200 6791,
ⓦwww.roadtrip.co.uk. Select from
the "North Wales and Snowdon" 3-day
tour or the "South Wales Horse-Riding"
weekend – both depart from London.
See Wales ℸ029/2022 7227,
ⓦwww.seewales.com. Minibus
sightseeing tours around Wales (1–5
days) for independent travellers and
small groups, with daily departures
from Cardiff.
Shaggy Sheep ℸ01267/281202 or
07919/244549, ⓦwww.shaggysheep
.com. Backpacker-oriented hop-on,
hop-off adventure tours, including
return transport from London.
Tracks Travel ℸ0845/130 0936,
ⓦwww.tracks-travel.com. Good-value
day-trips and weekend breaks to
Wales, including horse riding in the
Black Mountains and banquets at
Cardiff Castle.

△ Porth Dinllaen, Llŷn Peninsula

Southeast Wales

Home to some sixty percent of the country's population, Southeast Wales – the former heartland of the Welsh mining industry – is one of Britain's most industrialized regions. The nation's youthful capital, **Cardiff**, is a busy and entertaining place, but both population and industry are also heavily concentrated around the sea ports of **Newport** and **Swansea**, as well as inland along the **valleys**, where former coal mines have reopened as gutsy and hard-hitting museums.

Towards the English border, the beguiling **Wye Valley** provides a sylvan setting for **Tintern Abbey**, while to the west of Cardiff the beaches and quiet hills of the **Vale of Glamorgan**

make a peaceful escape. Further west still, the bays and cliffs of **Gower** are an essential detour from Swansea.

The Wye Valley

Crisscrossing between England and Wales, the River Wye cuts through the beguilingly rural countryside of the meandering **Wye Valley**. Make a beeline for the fortress town of **Chepstow**, its massive castle radiating an awesome strength; just to the north lie the inspirational ruins of the Cistercian **Tintern Abbey**, where there are beautiful walks through the surrounding bluebell woods and oak forests. Upstream, the old county town of **Monmouth** makes a gentle stop-off. The region becomes increasingly industrialized as you travel west; **Newport**, Wales's third-largest conurbation (granted city status in 2002), is unlikely to feature on a swift tour of Wales, but it has an excellent museum and the extensive remains of a Roman settlement in the northern suburb of Caerleon.

Chepstow

At the mouth of the River Wye, the fortress town of **CHEPSTOW** is the site of a spectacular **castle** (April, May & Oct daily 9.30am–5pm; June–Sept daily 9.30am–6pm; Nov–March Mon–Sat 9.30am–4pm, Sun 11am–4pm; £3.50; ⓦwww.cadw.wales.gov.uk), built tight into a loop of the Wye and comprising three separate enclosures. The mainly thirteenth-century **Lower Ward** holds the Great Hall, home to a wide-ranging exhibition on the castle's history. Twelfth-century defences separate the Lower Ward from the **Middle Ward**, which is dominated by the still imposing ruins of the Great Tower, whose lower floors include the original Norman keep. Beyond the Great Tower is the far narrower **Upper Ward** which leads up to the Barbican watch tower, from which there are some superlative views back over the castle and down to the mudflats of the river estuary.

Once you've exhausted the charms of Chepstow, you could follow the fairly challenging, two-hour **Wye Valley Walk** to Tintern Abbey (see below), which starts from the castle car park. A map (see ⓦwww.wyevalleywalk.org) – or an inexpensive leaflet available from the tourist office – is advisable, as the path meanders around and above the twisting Wye.

Chepstow: food and drink

Boat Inn The Back ☎01291/628192. A wonderfully convivial waterside pub with a good, vegetarian-friendly menu.
Five Alls Hocker Hill St ☎01291/630349. Genuine local inn with a friendly atmosphere and one of the best pub signs around.
Sitar Balti Beaufort Square ☎01291/627351. Excellent Indi-

an restaurant in the basement of a town house, specializing in balti lamb and chicken dishes.
Wye Knot The Back ☎01291/622929. Chepstow's finest, serving pricey gourmet meals on linen tablecloths adorned with fresh flowers. Good fish and vegetarian choices.

Tintern Abbey

Six miles north of Chepstow on one of the River Wye's most spectacular stretches, the roofless, ivy-clad ruins of **Tintern Abbey** (April, May & Oct daily 9.30am–5pm; June–Sept daily 9.30am–6pm; Nov–March Mon–Sat 9.30am–4pm, Sun 11am–4pm; £3.50 ⓦwww.cadw.wales.gov.uk) are genuinely uplifting. The "tall rock/The mountain, and the deep and gloomy wood" written about by Wordsworth are still evident today – particularly atmospheric if you visit early or late in the day and avoid the crowds. Founded as a monastic settlement in 1131, its buildings were plundered after dissolution, leaving the abbey to crumble into advanced decay. The centrepiece of the complex was the magnificent Gothic **church**, the bulk of which remains, with the remarkable tracery in the west window and intricate stonework of the capitals and columns firmly intact. Around the church are the less substantial ruins of the **monks' domestic quarters**, mostly reduced to one-storey rubble.

Immediately north of the abbey, **TINTERN** (Tyndyrn) has a **visitor centre** (April–Oct daily 10.30am–5.30pm; ☏01291/689566) at the **Old Station** complex where you can get leaflets on local walks. The charming *Cherry Tree*, half a mile up the road that forks off by the *Royal George Hotel*, has the best **beer** hereabouts, and also does great **food** and B&B.

Monmouth

Enclosed on three sides by the rivers Wye and Monnow, and retaining some quiet charm from its days as an important border post and one-time county town, **MONMOUTH** (Trefynwy) is centred on **Agincourt Square**, a handsome, cobbled open space dominated by old coaching inns, flanking the arched Georgian **Shire Hall**. From the square, you can walk up **Castle Hill** to peruse the ruins of the castle, founded in 1068, rebuilt in stone in the twelfth century and almost annihilated in the Civil War. The only notable part of the castle that remains is the Great Tower, in which Henry V is thought to have been born in 1387.

Nearby Monnow Street squeezes over the seven-hundred-year-old **Monnow Bridge**, crowned with a hulking stone gate of 1262 that served both as a means of defence for the town and a toll collection point. Just over a mile east of Monmouth, a steep road climbs up to **The Kymin** (daily dawn–dusk; free), a fine viewpoint over the town and the Wye Valley. It's crowned by the crenellated Georgian Round House and a Neoclassical **Naval Temple**, built in 1801 to celebrate Britain's victories at sea.

Monmouth: food and drink

Cygnet's Kitchen, in White Swan Court off Church Street, serves substantial soups and casseroles and has outside seating, while *The Maltsters*, 14 St Mary's Street, offers homemade muffins and cakes. Monmouth is home to a staggering number of **pubs**: worth trying are the *Green Dragon* on St Thomas Square, where you'll often get live music, or the *Robin Hood Inn*, on Monnow Street near the bridge, where Shakespeare is said to have drunk.

The Valleys

The Valleys is the generic name for the strings of settlements packed into narrow clefts in the mountainous terrain north of Newport, Cardiff and Swansea. They were once the coal- and iron-rich powerhouse of the nation, and represent the Wales of popular imagination: hemmed-in valley floors crowded with lines of blank, grey houses, their doors and sills painted in contrasting gaudy brightness, slanted almost impossibly towards the pithead. Although nearly all of the mines have now closed, the area is still tight-knit, with a rich working-class heritage that displays itself in some excellent museums and colliery tours.

Blaenafon and Big Pit

With its lofty hillside position, **BLAENAFON** has a far less claustrophobic feel than many valley towns. A fascinating and evocative place, it gained UNESCO World Heritage Site status in 2000, and the town's Victorian boom can be seen in its architecture, most notably the impressively florid **Working Men's Hall** that dominates the town centre.

Three-quarters of a mile west of the town, and accessible by half-hourly shuttle bus from Blaenafon, the **Big Pit National Coal Museum** (daily: Feb–Nov 9.30am–5pm; Dec & Jan 10am–4.30pm; last underground tour 3.30pm; free ☎01495/790311 ⓦwww.museumwales.ac.uk) provides a consummate picture of a miner's work and life; many of the guides are ex-miners. Kitted out with lamp, helmet and very heavy battery-pack, you descend 300ft into the labyrinth of shafts and coal faces. Constant streams of rust-coloured water flow by, adding to the dank and chilly atmosphere that must have terrified the small children who pulled the coal wagons along the tracks, working a six-day week for twopence (of which one penny was subtracted for the cost of their candles).

On the rolling moorland by the entrance of the pit, the old mine train line has been brought back into partial use as the **Pontypool and Blaenafon Steam Railway** (Easter–early Oct Sat, Sun & bank holidays 11.30am–4.30pm; £2.50), worth taking for the couple of hundred yards to the evocative *Whistle Inn*, once the main pub for the miners, but now dependent on tourists. The atmosphere is unashamedly nostalgic, with a collection of miners' tin lamps hanging from the ceiling.

Caerphilly

Seven miles north of Cardiff at the foot of the Rhymney Valley, **CAERPHILLY** (Caerffili) is worth visiting for its **castle** (April, May & Oct daily 9.30am–5pm; June–Sept daily 9.30am–6pm; Nov–March Mon–Sat 9.30am–4pm, Sun 11am–4pm; £3.50 ⓦwww.cadw.wales.gov.uk), with an inner system of defences overlooking the outer ring, all looming above a vast moat. You enter through a great **gatehouse** that punctures the barbican wall, much restored and now housing an exhibition about the castle's history. From here, a bridge crosses the moat to the outer wall of the castle itself, behind which sits the hulking Inner Ward. On the left is the south-eastern tower, outleaning its rival in Pisa and with a great cleft in its walls where Cromwell's men are said to have attempted to blow it up. Also interesting is the massive eastern gatehouse, which includes an impressive upper hall and oratory and, to its left, the wholly restored and re-roofed **Great Hall**, largely built around 1317 by Hugh le Despenser.

△ Caerphilly Castle

Despite its famous crumbly white cheese, Caerphilly isn't noted for its **eating**; the *Courthouse* inn, overlooking the castle on Cardiff Road, serves predictable pub grub; or head to *Glanmor's Tearooms*, across from the castle in the shopping precinct, for the town's best Caerphilly Welsh Rarebit (cheese-on-toast).

The Rhondda

The Rhondda starts just outside Pontypridd, winding through the mountains alongside train line, road and river for a few miles to **TREHAFOD**. Here you'll find the area's main attraction, the colliery museum of the **Rhondda Heritage Park** (April–Sept daily 10am–6pm; Oct–March Tues–Sun 10am–6pm; last tour 4pm; £5.60 ⓦwww.rhonddaheritagepark.com), formed by locals when the Lewis Merthyr Colliery closed in 1983. You can explore the engine winding houses, lamp room, fan house and a simulated "trip underground", with stunning visuals and sound effects, re-creating 1950s and late nineteenth-century life (and death) through the eyes of colliers. A chilling roll-call of pit deaths and a final narration by ex–Labour Party leader Neil Kinnock about the human cost of mining – especially for the Valley women – are very moving. The Heritage Park is a five-minute walk from Trehafod **train station**.

Cardiff

With its beautifully regenerated waterfront and fabulous national sports stadium, the buoyant city of **CARDIFF** (Caerdydd) boasts the true feel of an international capital. There's plenty to see and do, but the city's great asset is its terrific energy, something that no one who wants to enjoy Wales should miss.

The commercial centre

Compact and easily navigable on foot, Cardiff's **commercial centre** is bounded by the River Taff – source of the nickname of generations of expatriate Welsh – on the western side. The Taff flows past the walls of Cardiff's extraordinary **castle** (daily: March–Oct 9.30am–6pm; Nov–Feb 9.30am–5pm; last admission 1hr before closing; £7.50, grounds only £3.75), an amalgam of Roman remains, Norman keep and Victorian fantasy. Nearby is the great 74,500-seat **Millennium Stadium** (tours hourly Mon–Sat 10am–5pm, Sun 10am–4pm, subject to events; £5.50 ⓦwww.millenniumstadium.com). Home of Welsh rugby and the nation's soccer team, as well as serving as a venue for a host of major rock gigs and other musical spectaculars, it's an iconic symbol not only of Cardiff, but of Wales as a whole. Tours take in the players' tunnel, dressing rooms, VIP areas and a rugby museum.

Near the southeastern tip of the castle walls is Cardiff's main crossroads, where the Edwardian boulevards of Queen Street and High Street conceal a world of arcades and great shopping. The **High Street** and **Castle arcades**, at the top of High Street, are the most rewarding, packed with great clubwear shops, quirky gift places, fab little coffee-houses and a range of esoteric emporia where you can pick up fliers for clubs and events. Further down the High Street towards Central Station, the glorious Morgan Arcade and the Royal Arcade run east to the bottom of **The Hayes**, a pedestrianized street of disparate restaurants and some great pubs. Slicing off south, opposite the *Marriott* hotel, is cheerful Mill Lane, Cardiff's self-proclaimed **café quarter**.

Cathays Park and the National Museum and Gallery

North of the castle are the grand Edwardian buildings and green spaces of the civic centre in **Cathays Park**. Centrepiece of the complex is the magnificent, domed, dragon-topped **City Hall**, whose showy first-floor Marble Hall holds statues of Welsh heroes such as Owain Glyndŵr and Dewi Sant – the national patron saint, St David.

Beside City Hall, the **National Museum and Gallery** (Tues–Sun & bank hols 10am–5pm; free ⓦwww.museumwales. ac.uk) is one of Britain's finest, telling the story of Wales and reflecting the nation's place in the wider, international sphere. The most obvious crowd-pleaser is the epic **Evolution of Wales** gallery, a natural-history exhibition packed with high-tech gizmos and a staggering amount of information. The real highlights, though, are the **art galleries**, with everything from first-century BC marble altars illustrating Wales's artistic heritage to an important collection from the eighteenth-century British and Italian schools, including works by Welshmen Richard Wilson, William E. Parry and Thomas Jones, and a superb collection of **ceramics**, one of Wales's most prolific areas of applied art. The most exciting works are contained in galleries Eleven to Fifteen; don't miss the fabulous **sculpture** collection, including home-grown pieces by Goscombe John, while Gallery Thirteen houses the museum's impressive collection of **Impressionists** – works by Cézanne, Degas, Pissarro and Van Gogh.

Cardiff Bay and around

A mile south of the commercial centre is **Cardiff Bay**, revitalized since the construction of a barrage to form a vast freshwater lake and eight miles of smartly regenerated waterfront. Get there by waterbus (from The Taff Mead Embankment), train (every 15min from Queen Street station) or bendy-bus (every 10–15 mins from Central station).

The waterfront's latest additions are the mesmerizingly graceful **Wales Millennium Centre** (ⓦwww.wmc.org.uk), a suitable home for the internationally renowned Welsh National Opera, and the award-winning Senedd Building, new home to the Welsh Assembly.

Further west around the waterfront, the metal-and-glass-crowned **Techniquest**, on Stuart Street (Mon–Fri 9.30am–4.30pm, Sat & Sun 10.30am–5pm; £6.90 ⓦwww.techniquest .org), is one of the largest and most impressive "hands-on" science museums in the UK, packed full of exhibits, experiments and numerous chances to play like a five-year-old. It also includes a planetarium (£1.20 extra) and science theatre.

Built across the Ely and Taff estuaries, the kilometre-long **Cardiff Bay Barrage** (daily 8am–8pm; Nov–March closes 4pm; free) is a phenomenal piece of engineering, and its walls, lock gates, sluices and fish path are well worth exploring. To find out about what's going on in the area, visit the **Cardiff Bay Visitor Centre** on Harbour Drive (Mon–Fri 9.30am–6pm, Sat & Sun 10.30am–6pm; Oct–March closes 5pm; free), a startling, giant tubular eye peering out over the bay, which contains a scale model of the entire docks area, illuminated to show different infrastructure developments. Directly behind the centre, **Bay Island Voyages** (operates throughout the year (weather dependent); ☏01446/420 692) offer various boat trips including high-adrenaline cruises around the bay.

△ Cardiff Bay

Museum of Welsh Life

Four miles west of Cardiff in the small village of St Fagans, the massively popular **Museum of Welsh Life** (daily 10am–5pm; free ⓦwww.museumwales.ac.uk) tells the country's history through bricks and mortar, with a sundry collection of buildings salvaged from all over Wales. The most impressive are the diminutive whitewashed 1777 **Pen-Rhiw Chapel** from Dyfed, the pristine and evocative Victorian **St Mary's Board School** from Lampeter and the ordered mini-fortress of a 1772 **Tollhouse** that once guarded the southern approach to Aberystwyth. It's also worth nosing round the superlative **Rhyd-y-car** ironworkers' cottages from Merthyr Tydfil, originally built around 1800 and each furnished in the style of a different era – stretching from 1805 to 1985. Next door, jars of boiled sweets are sold by starchy-aproned assistants at the Victorian **Gwalia Stores**.

Buses #32 and #320 operate at least hourly to St Fagans from Cardiff Central station.

Cardiff: food

Cardiff's long-standing internationalism – particularly its Italian influence – has paid handsome dividends in a broad range of **restaurants**. Most places are within easy walking distance of the city centre, with a particular concentration in the "Café Quarter" around Mill Lane. There are also good options in the cheaper corners of Cathays and Roath (particularly the curry houses along Crwys, Albany and City roads), a stone's throw from the centre beyond the university.

Armless Dragon 97 Wyverne Rd, Cathays ☎029/2038 2357. Unusual and enjoyable place, with a good range of Welsh dishes, generally served with some delicious twist, all moderate to expensive in price. Closed Sun.

Celtic Cauldron Castle Arcade. Inexpensive, friendly daytime café dedicated to bringing a range of simple Welsh food – soups, stews, laver bread, cakes – to an appreciative public.

Cibo 83 Pontcanna St, off Cathedral Rd ☎029/2023 2226. Serving ciabatta sandwiches, pizza, pasta and a blackboard of simple, well-cooked daily specials, this small, moderately priced trattoria provides a slice of Italy in Cardiff.

Clarks Pie Shops 454 Cowbridge Road East ☎029/2056 2697. Cardiff's best loved snack straight from the oven. A sister shop is located on Bromsgrove Street.

Juboraj II 10 Mill Lane. One of Cardiff's best South Asian restaurants, yet still moderately priced – great for quality Indian art and raga music with your thali. Closed Sun.

La Brasserie 60 St Mary St ☎029/2037 2164. Popular French eaterie that does very tasty food and can be huge fun.

Fabulous Welshcakes Mermaid Quay, Cardiff Bay ☎029/2051 2443. Freshly baked Welshcakes

in a variety of flavours.
Madeira 2 Guildford Crescent, off Churchill Way ☎029/2066 7705. Enjoyable Portuguese restaurant, great for skewers of meat and other carnivorous delights. Good-value set menu at lunchtime.
Mimosa Kitchen & Bar Mermaid Quay, Cardiff Bay ☎029/2049 1900. Quality Welsh produce with a good selection of vegetarian dishes.
Norwegian Church Café Harbour Drive, Cardiff Bay. Cosy spot for Norwegian open sandwiches, salads, scrumptious cakes and good coffee.

Cardiff: drink

Cardiff's **pub** life has expanded exponentially in recent years, with chic, cosmopolitan **bars** starting to displace the more traditional Edwardian palaces of etched glass and red wood. Don't forget Cardiff's own beer, **Brains**, whose Bitter is pale and refreshing and whose Dark is a deep mild that should not be missed on a visit to its home city.

Cayo Arms Cathedral Rd. Proudly Welsh pub, 5min walk up Cathedral Rd from the city centre, with Tomos Watkin beers and decent food every day until 8pm.
Chapter Market Rd, Canton. A trendy bar in the arts centre, with a good choice of real ale and whisky. Frequented by the Canton media and arts crowd.

The Cottage 25 St Mary St. A traditional Edwardian pub, serving up some of the best Brains in the city centre, as well as cheap food.
Ha-ha Bar The Friary. Decent posing palace in town, an enjoyable, young and funky place that also serves great food.

Cardiff: nightlife

Cardiff's burgeoning **club** and **dance** scene is extraordinarily diverse and popular. Club nights change frequently: check online to find out what's going on.

Barfly Kingsway ⓦwww.barflyclub .com. Dark and sweaty club near the castle that hosts at least a couple of live bands each evening.

Clwb Ifor Bach 11 Womanby St ⓦwww.clwb.net. Sweaty and fun live-music and dance club on three floors, with nightly gigs, sessions or DJs. Widely regarded as the city's greatest supporter and purveyor of Welsh-language acts.

Metros Bakers Row. Grungey, scruffy venue that hosts some of the best indie/alternative dance nights in town, with lots of students drawn by the drink promotions.

Minskys Cathedral Walk ⓦwww.minskys-showbar.com. Unique live entertainment venue renowned for outrageous caberet

Royal Oak 200 Broadway, Newport Rd, Roath ⓦwww.royaloakcardiff.co.uk. Live-music pub, with something of a fetish for boxing memorabilia – there's even an old boxing ring.

Toucan 95 Newport Rd ⓦwww.toucanclub.co.uk. Hip-hop, jazz, world music and funk are the main menu of this Cardiff institution.

The Union 3 Churchill Way ⓦwww.cardiffstudents.com. Big-name live bands and assorted dance nights in this impressive university club complex, open to non-students.

The Vale of Glamorgan

The bowl of land in the very south of Wales is known as the **Vale of Glamorgan**, a rich, pastoral land of gentle countryside shelving down to a cliff-ridden coastline, punctuated by long, sandy beaches. Most visitors speed straight from Cardiff to Swansea missing the Vale's quiet, pretty towns, and its profusion of excellent beaches and tumbledown castles. Brash seaside resorts at **Porthcawl** in the west and **Barry** to the east contrast with the more refined, breezy atmosphere of **Penarth**, a prim seaside town clinging to the coat-tails of Cardiff. In between lie yawning wide bays and spectacular ruins, linked by bracing coastal walks. Southwest of Cardiff, **Dyffryn Gardens** (April–Oct daily 10am–6pm; £6; Nov–March Thurs–Mon 11am–4pm; £3 ⓦwww.dyffryngardens.org.uk) offer everything from formal lily-ponds to joyous bursts of floral colour and the russets and greens of an arboretum, all set around a Victorian merchant's home.

Swansea

In 1947, local boy Dylan Thomas called **SWANSEA** (Abertawe) an "ugly, lovely town". Sprawling and boisterous, it remains Wales's second city – but is the undoubted Welsh capital of attitude.

Swansea is far more of a Welsh town than Cardiff, and you'll hear *yr iaith Gymraeg*, the Welsh language, spoken daily on its streets. It is also undergoing something of a renaissance, with resurgent music, club and surf scenes, a stunning new museum and some spirited redesigns of streets and squares in the centre.

The city's highlights include the spacious and graceful suburb of **Uplands** (a wide seafront overlooking the huge sweep of Swansea Bay), and a bold marina development around the old **South Docks**. At the latter, the enticingly old-fashioned **Swansea Museum** (Tues–Sun 10.00am–5.00pm; free) is surrounded by nineteenth-century streets that have been thoughtfully gentrified, and now house some enjoyable cafés, pubs and restaurants. Tucked behind the museum is the **Dylan Thomas Centre** (daily 10am–4.30pm; free ⓦwww.dylanthomas.com), with a theatre space, two galleries, a restaurant, bookshops and craft shops, as well as an extensive display on Dylan Thomas himself.

At the marina, the sublime **National Waterfront Museum** (daily 10am–5pm; free ⓦwww.museumwales.ac.uk) boasts fifteen exhibition zones dedicated to Wales's history that are bursting with spectacular interactive technology. Nearby on Gloucester Place is the mural-splattered warehouse housing the **Dylan Thomas Theatre**, which intersperses productions of his work with visiting and local companies' offerings.

Swansea's **market** – its curving roof sheltering underneath the Quadrant Centre – makes a lively sight, with plenty of colourful stalls and the smells of flowers and fresh baking. On sale are local delicacies such as laver bread, a delicious savoury made from seaweed, as well as cockles trawled from the nearby Loughor estuary, typical Welsh cakes, fish and cheeses.

Swansea: food, drink and fun

Swansea is a city that knows how to have a good time, and provides plenty of opportunities to do so. Dozens of new **bars** and **restaurants** have emerged in recent years. Wind Street is the city's main booze artery, with brasher, younger clubs ranged around Kingsway.

Restaurants and cafés

Chelsea Café 17 St Mary St
℡01792/464068. Local ingre-

dients served with flair and imagination are the staples of

Surfing

The best **surfing** spots in Wales are undoubtedly on the south-west-facing beaches. The most notable waves can be found on the Gower Peninsula at **Llangennith**, situated at the northern end of Rhossili Bay. The area is growing in popularity as a prime Welsh surfing spot - famous for the consistent swells that pour in from the Atlantic Ocean. Other great spots are dotted all along the Peninsula coastline. Caswell Bay is convenient for those staying in Swansea. The beach at Rhossili is vast and great for experienced riders, while Horton and Port Eynon both have quality waves when the big South West swells come in, but generally have more gentle waves, perfect for beginners. Beginner's lessons are available from several schools, including **SurfGSD** (℡01792 360 370, ⓦwww.gowersurfing.com) and the **Welsh Surfing Federation Surf School** (℡01792 386426, ⓦwww.wsfsurfschool.co.uk). Up-to-date surf condition reports for Llangennith can be found at ⓦwww.gowerlive.co.uk.

this place, Welsh with a touch of France.

Govinda's 8 Craddock St. ☎01792/468469. Vegetarian restaurant in the Hare Krishna tradition, selling very cheap meals and freshly squeezed juices.

New Capriccio 89 St Helen's Rd ☎01792/648804. Popular Italian restaurant with a bargain lunch menu. Closed Sun evening & Mon.

Street Pebble Café Bar 11 Wind St. Wicker, stones and a candlelit interior provide a chilled ambience – great for morning smoothies, daytime paninis or Mediterranean food in the evenings.

Bars, pubs and clubs

Celtic Pride 49 Uplands Crescent, Uplands. Good local pub with almost nightly live music, including jam sessions and Welsh music.

Escape Club Northampton Lane, off Kingsway ⓦwww.escape-group.com. Enormous, purpose-built dance venue that pulls big-name DJs for a dizzying array of club nights.

Ice Bar 64 Wind St. One of the trendier Wind Street establishments, loud and lively at all times.

Monkey Café 13 Castle St ⓦwww.monkeycafe.co.uk. Groovy, inexpensive, mosaic-floored café with a relaxed atmosphere and nightly DJs or live music.

No Sign Bar 56 Wind St. A narrow frontage leads into a long, warm pub interior, one of the oldest in town and easily the best on this street.

Palace 156 High St. Two-room club that vies with *Escape* for the most hardcore tunes, but beats it hands down for atmosphere.

Gower

A fifteen-mile peninsula of undulating limestone, **GOWER** (Gŵyr) juts into the Bristol Channel to the west of Swansea. The area is fringed by sweeping yellow bays and precipitous cliffs, caves and blowholes to the south, and wide, flat marshes and cockle beds to the north. Bracken-covered heaths with prehistoric remains and tiny villages lie between, with castle ruins and curious churches spread evenly around.

Mumbles and Oystermouth

At the far westernmost end of Swansea Bay and on the cusp of Gower, lively and enjoyable **MUMBLES** (Mwmbwls) offers a diverse range of seaside entertainment, fine restaurants and the legendary **Mumbles Mile** of pubs – best bets are the *Antelope*, and *White Rose*. "Mumbles" is now also used to refer to the entire sprawl of **OYSTERMOUTH** (Ystumllwynarth); the two names are used pretty much interchangeably. Here, the seafront is an unbroken curve of budget hotels, breezy pubs and cafés leading down to the old-fashioned pier and funfair towards the rocky plug of Mumbles Head. Behind the promenade, a busy warren of streets climb the hills, lined with souvenir shops, department stores and a glut of fine restaurants. Around the headland lies **Langland Bay**, with a sandy beach popular with **surfers**.

Food highlights include the inexpensive *Coffee Denn*, 34 Newton Rd, particularly good for sweet treats, while the moderately priced *P.A.'s Wine Bar*, 95 Newton Rd, does a very reasonable line in hearty Welsh cooking. Best of all is *Verdi's*, overlooking the sea at Knab Rock near the pier – a Mumbles institution for its lively Welsh–Italian atmosphere, superb pizza and ice-cream concoctions.

Mumbles Head to Three Cliffs Bay

The first few miles of the southern Gower coast are highly developed, with stern hotels and beach huts backing some fine sands. Head along the stunning cliff path past Langland Bay and the narrow, golden-sanded Caswell Bay to the tiny and remote old smugglers' haunt of **Brandy Cove**, or pebbly **Pwll Du Bay**, which is owned by the National Trust and backed by a wooded ravine that offers many stunning walks.

Three miles along, huge **Three Cliffs Bay** is one of Gower's finest beaches, a silent valley fringed by dunes and overlooked by the eerie ruins of **Pennard Castle**. Although justifiably popular, its relative inaccessibility ensures that it's never packed. The best approach is from the car park at **Southgate**, from where you hike a mile or so west along cliff tops inhabited by

△ Three Cliffs Bay

semi-wild ponies to the bay itself. Here, you can turn inland and follow the boundary of the golf course to reach the castle.

Rhossili and Worms Head

At the western end of the Gower, the village of **RHOS-SILI** (Rhosili) is a centre for walkers and beach loungers alike. Dylan Thomas described the terrain to the west as "rubbery, gull-limed grass, the sheep-pilled stones, the pieces of bones and feathers", and you can tread in his footsteps to **Worms Head**, an isolated string of rocks with the spectacular appearance of a basking Welsh dragon, accessible for only five hours around low tide: times are available from the National Trust visitor centre (April–Oct daily 10.30am–5pm; Nov & Dec Wed–Sun 11am–4pm; Jan–March Thurs–Sun 11am–4pm; ☎01792/390707) at the head of the road, near the village.

The **food** at the *Worms Head Hotel*, by the car park, is no more than OK, but there is no pub garden in Wales with a finer view.

Southwest Wales

S outhwest Wales attracts thousands of visitors each year, mainly for the fabulous scenery; bucolic and magical inland, sweeping and flat around Carmarthen Bay and rocky, indented and spectacular further west. Approaching from Swansea, the **National Botanic Garden**, **Aberglasney** with its magnficent formal grounds and the stronghold of

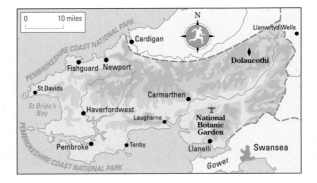

Carreg Cennan Castle are all worthwhile detours en route to Dylan Thomas's final home in **Laugharne**. The picturesque town of **Tenby** heralds the wonderful **Pembrokeshire Coast National Park**, centred on the tiny city of **St Davids** and ringed by a 186-mile **Coast Path**. Virtually the entire coast from Tenby to Cardigan is inside the national park.

The National Botanic Garden of Wales

Seven miles east of the town of Carmarthen lies the great glass "eye" of the **National Botanic Garden of Wales** (daily: Easter–Oct 10am–6pm; Nov–Easter 10am–4.30pm; £8; ⓦwww.gardenofwales.org.uk), designed around the principles of sustainability. A central walkway leads past lakes, sculpture and geological outcrops, while on the estate's outer edges are re-creations of moorland, spring wood, prairie and native Welsh habitats. The garden's most audacious feature is the vast, stunning oval **glasshouse** designed by Norman Foster, holding plants from all over the world. Bus #166 runs to the garden from Carmarthen station.

If you're in the area, drop in to the *White Hart* in Llanddarog, near the garden – a thatched pub that brews its own beer – or try the superb ales at the unpretentious *Drovers Arms* on Lammas Street in the centre of Carmarthen.

Aberglasney

A natural twin to the nearby Botanic Garden, **Aberglasney** (daily: April–Sept 10am–6pm; Oct–March 10.30am–4pm; £6.50 ⓦwww.aberglasney.org) is a restored manor house that was nearly demolished after assorted parts (even the eight-columned portico) were put up for auction. The building was saved but is overshadowed by its magnificent formal grounds. Once massively overgrown, these sixteenth- to eighteenth-century walled gardens have regained much of their splendour, and archeological work continues to uncover more about the history of the site.

Carreg Cennen Castle

Isolated in the rural hinterland southeast of Aberglasney, and three miles from the nearest bus-stop (in Llandeilo), **Carreg Cennen Castle** (daily: April–Oct 9.30am–6.30pm; Nov–March 9.30am–4pm; £3.50 ⓦwww.cadw.wales.gov.uk) is the most magnificently sited castle in Wales, three hundred feet

△ Carreg Cennen Castle

above a sheer drop into the green valley of the Cennen River, its crumbling walls merging with the limestone on which it defiantly sits. The highlights of a visit are the views down into the valley and the long descent into a watery, pitch-black **cave** that is said to have served as a well. Torches are essential, and can be rented for 50p from the tearoom near the car park, which also has a superb selection of home-made Welsh **food**. A mile below the castle in the village of Trap, the *Cennen Arms* is a good spot for a **drink**.

Dolaucothi

North of Llandeilo, near the straggling village of Pumsaint (Five Saints), the **Dolaucothi Gold Mine** (April–Oct 10am–5pm; £3.40, underground tour £3.80 extra) offers a unique insight into Welsh gold mining, from early extraction by the Romans to the industrialized workings of the nineteenth and early twentieth centuries. Gold panning and underground tours are widely touted but the site's main appeal is the mass of 1930s mining machinery set in the bucolic Cothi Valley.

Laugharne

With a ragged castle looming over the reeds and tidal flats of the Taf estuary southwest of Carmarthen, and narrow lanes snuggling in behind, **LAUGHARNE** (Talacharn) is a delightful village, increasingly overtaken by the legend of Dylan Thomas. The **Dylan Thomas Boathouse** (daily: Easter & May–Oct 10am–5.30pm; Nov–April 10.30am–3.30pm; £3 ⓦwww.dylanthomasboathouse.com) was the simple home of Thomas and his family from 1949 until he died from "a massive insult to the brain" (spurred by numerous whiskies) in New York four years later. Nowadays it's an enchanting and inspirational museum above the ever-changing water and light of the estuary and its "heron-priested shore". The family's living room has been preserved intact, with the rich tones of the man himself reading his work via a period wireless set. You can also peer into the blue garage where Thomas wrote: scrunched-up balls of paper on the cheap desk suggesting that he might return at any minute.

Thomas and his wife Caitlin, who died in 1994, are buried together in the graveyard of the **parish church** in the village centre, marked by a simple white cross. Literary pilgrims might also want to have a drink at his old boozing hole, **Brown's Hotel** on the main street, where, in the nicotine-crusted front bar, Dylan's cast-iron table still sits in a window alcove.

Laugharne has several good places to **eat**. For lunches and Welsh teas make for the *Pea Green Boat* on the central square, while for something more substantial try the *Stable Door* on Market Lane (☎01994/427777; closed Mon–Wed), a relaxed restaurant and wine bar with an upmarket menu. Down on the square, plump for tasty fish-and-chips at the *Castle View*. The best **pub** is the cheery *New Three Mariners*.

Tenby

Wedged between its sweeping north and south beaches, and fronting an island-studded seascape, beguilingly old-fashioned **TENBY** (Dinbych-y-Pysgod) is everything a seaside resort should be. Narrow streets duck and wind downhill from the medieval centre to the harbour. Steps down the steeper slopes provide magical views of the dockside arches which still house fishmongers selling the morning's catch, while rows of brightly painted houses and hotels are strung along the clifftops.

The focal point of Tenby's old centre is the 152-foot spire of the largely fifteenth-century **St Mary's Church**, bordered

△ Tenby Harbour

on its western side by Upper Frog Street, complete with craft shops and an arcaded indoor **market**, containing craft stalls and gift shops.

Sheltered by the curving headland and fringed by pastel-hued Georgian and Victorian houses, Tenby's **harbour** is a great place to stroll on a warm evening, as well as being the departure point for trips to **Caldey Island** (Ynys Pyr), which looms large on the horizon a few miles offshore. Boats leave every twenty minutes in season (Easter–Oct Mon–Sat approx 10am–4pm; £8 return; ☎01834 844453 ⓦwww.caldey-island. co.uk) for the twenty-minute journey to the island, where you can tour the garish twentieth-century **monastery** – a white, turreted pile resembling a Disney castle – and explore the priory and its twelfth-century **St Illtud's Church**.

Tenby: food and drink

Café 25 25 High St. Espresso bar with freshly-baked pastries and internet access upstairs.

Coach and Horses Upper Frog St. Animated, wood-beamed pub popular with a young crowd who appreciate the good beer and tasty Thai food.

Fecci and Sons Upper Frog St. Italian snack-bar and ice-cream parlour, with over sixty speciality ice creams.

Lifeboat Tavern Tudor Square.

Popular and easygoing pub, with a youthful clientele.

Plantagenet House Quay Hill ☎01834/842350. Cosy, expensive and thoroughly enjoyable restaurant serving local specialities. The building is the oldest house in Tenby – notice the massive tenth-century Flemish chimney en route to the loo.

Reef Café St Julian St. Mediterranean-themed bistro, with excellent-value snacks at lunchtime.

The Pembrokeshire Coast National Park

Of the twelve national parks in England and Wales, the **Pembrokeshire Coast National Park** (ⓦwww.pcnpa.org .uk) is the only one that is predominantly sea-based, hugging the rippled coastline around the entire southwestern section of Wales. Established in 1952, the park is not one easily identifiable mass, rather a series of occasionally unconnected patches of coast and inland scenery.

Starting at its southeastern corner, the first segment clings to the coast from **Amroth** through to the **Milford Haven** waterway, an area of sweeping limestone cliffs and some fabulous beaches. The second (and by far the quietest) part courses around the inland pastoral landscape of the **Daugleddau Estuary**, which plunges deep into the rural heart of Pembrokeshire southeast of Haverfordwest. Superb for scenic cliff walking, the third section is around the beaches and resorts of **St Bride's Bay**, where the sea scoops a great chunk out of Wales's westernmost land. In the north of the county, the boundary of the park runs far inland to encompass the **Mynydd Preseli**, a barren but invigoratingly beautiful range of hills dotted with ancient relics.

The Pembrokeshire Coast Path

Crawling around almost every wriggle of this coast, the **Pembrokeshire Coast Path** winds 186 miles from Amroth in the south to its northernmost point at St Dogmael's near Cardigan. The path generally clings precariously to clifftop routes, overlooking rocks frequented by sunbathing seals, craggy offshore islands, unexpected gashes of sand and shrieking clouds of sea birds.

The **best places to walk** are around St Davids Head and the Marloes Peninsula, either side of St Bride's Bay; the stretch from the castle at Manorbier to the tiny cliff chapel at Bosherston along the southern coast; and the undulating contours, massive cliffs, bays and old ports along the northern coast, either side of Fishguard.

Barafundle Bay to Freshwater West

The southern zigzag of coast that darts west from Tenby is a strange mix of caravan parks and Ministry of Defence shooting ranges above some spectacularly beautiful bays and gull-covered cliffs. Half a mile west along the Coast Path from the tiny, picturesque harbour of Stackpole Quay, south of Pembroke, **Barafundle Bay** is one of the finest beaches in Europe, with clear water and soft sand fringed by wooded cliffs. Push on along the Coast Path, past the compact beach at Broad Haven, and you'll reach a spot overlooking the cliffs where **St Govan's Chapel** is wedged. This tiny grey structure is at least eight hundred (and possibly as much as fourteen hundred) years old.

△ St. Govan's Chapel

Legend has it that St Govan chose this spot to be buried after hoodlums attacked him on the clifftop and the cliffs opened up and folded gently around him, saving him from certain death. Steps descend into the sandy-floored chapel and to a small cell hewn from the rock, containing the fissure that reputedly sheltered Govan. In the nearby village of Bosherston, the enjoyable *St Govan's Country Inn* serves inexpensive food and real ales.

After an inland spell, the Coast Path returns to the sea at **Freshwater West**, a west-facing beach resort that's great for surfing, though the currents can be too strong for swimming. Behind the beach, desolate wind-battered dunes make for interesting walking.

St Bride's Bay and the Islands

The most westerly point of Wales – and the very furthest you can get from England – is one of the country's most enchanting areas. The coast around **St Bride's Bay** is broken into rocky outcrops, islands and broad, sweeping beaches curving around between two headlands that sit like giant crab pincers reaching out into the warm Gulf Stream waters of the crashing Atlantic.

Skomer and Skokholm

Reached by boats from Martin's Haven (April–Oct Tues–Sun & bank hols 10am, 11am & noon; £14; ⓦwww.dale-sailing .co.uk), **Skomer** is a 722-acre flat-topped island known as one of the finest **sea-bird** colonies in northern Europe. Puffins, gulls, guillemots, storm petrels, cormorants, shags and kittiwakes all abound, but most celebrated are the 200,000-plus Manx shearwaters. Skomer also harbours the remains of hundreds of ancient hut circles, collapsed defensive ramparts and a Bronze Age standing stone known as Harold's Stone, near where the boats land. In spring and early summer, wild flowers carpet the island, and in autumn grey seals bask at the northern end.

You can also see the island by way of non-landing, **round-Skomer cruises** (April–Oct daily inc bank hols 1pm, Mon when not bank hol also 10am & 11.30am; £8); the summertime evening cruises are great for spotting sea birds (May–July Tues, Wed & Fri 7pm; £10).

Two miles south of Skomer, the warm red sandstone cliffs of the 240-acre island of **Skokholm** make a sharp contrast to Skomer's grey severity. Britain's first bird observatory was founded here in the 1930s, and the island is still rich in birdlife. The cruises outlined above circle Skokholm, or you could call the local Wildlife Trust (℡01239/621600) for details of staying overnight on either island.

St Davids

Founded – according to tradition – by the Welsh patron saint himself in 550 AD, **ST DAVIDS** (Tyddewi) is one of the most enchanting and evocative spots in Britain. This miniature city clusters around its cathedral at the westernmost point of Wales on a windswept, treeless peninsula of awesome ruggedness. The country's spiritual and ecclesiastical centre, St Davids was granted official city status in 1995.

St Davids High Street courses down to the triangular Cross Square, with its centrepiece **Celtic cross**, and continues under

Coasteering

Developed in the 1980s in Pembrokeshire's St Davids Peninsula, **coasteering** is an exhilarating multi-sport combination of scrambling over rocks, jumping off cliffs and swimming across narrow bays. It's suitable for just about anyone (even non-swimmers). Top operators include TYF (℡01437/721611, www.tyf.com) and Preseli Venture (℡01348/837709, www.preseliventure.co.uk). Also see www.adventure.visitwales.com

△ Coasteering, St Non's

the thirteenth-century **Tower Gate**, which forms the entrance to Cathedral Close. The gold-and-purple 125-foot stone tower of **St Davids Cathedral** itself (daily 9am–7pm; donation requested; ⓦwww.stdavidscathedral.org.uk) is topped by pert golden pinnacles that seem to glow a different colour from the rest of the building. You enter via a porch in the south side of the low twelfth-century nave. Highlights inside include the tower's magnificently bold and bright **lantern ceiling** and, at the back of the right-hand choir stalls, a unique **monarch's stall** – unlike any other British cathedral, the Queen is automatically a member of the St Davids Cathedral Chapter. The **misericords** under the choir seats display earthy medieval humour; there's one of a chaotic wild-boar hunt and another of someone being seasick.

Behind the filled-in lancets at the back of the presbytery altar is the Perpendicular **Bishop Vaughan's Chapel**, crafted out of a soft honeyed stone, with an exquisite fan tracery roof built between 1508 and 1522. Behind the chapel is the ambulatory, off which leads the simple **Lady Chapel**, with some sentimental Edwardian stained glass.

Guided tours of the cathedral (July & Aug Mon, Tues, Thurs & Fri 2.30pm; £4) are arranged at the bookshop in the nave. Also worth noting is the cathedral's superb annual **music festival** which takes place in late May/early June.

From the cathedral, a path leads over the River Alun to the splendid fourteenth-century **Bishop's Palace** (April, May & Oct daily 9.30am–5pm; June–Sept daily 9.30am–6pm; Nov–March Mon–Sat 9.30am–4pm, Sun 11am–4pm; £2.90). Its huge central quadrangle is enclosed by an array of ruined buildings, notably the impressive **Bishops' Hall** and the enormous **Great Hall**, with its glorious rose window. Beneath the Great Hall are dank vaults containing an interesting exhibition about the palace and the indulgent lifestyles of its occupants.

St Davids: food and drink

With only one **pub** to its name, St Davids might appear to be a backwater. Not so: the city is a real magnet for surfers, outdoor types and musicians. In summer, and over Christmas/New Year, parties are likely to break out just about anywhere. It's also a great place to eat, with **restaurants** for all tastes and budgets.

Bench 11 High St ⓦ www.bench-bar.co.uk. Classy but relaxed restaurant, café and wine bar. Pop in for a quick espresso and panini or to linger over pizza and great Italian ice cream.

Cwtch 22 High Street ☎01437/720491. Relaxed, homely environment serving fresh local produce.

Farmers Arms Goat St. The city's only real pub. Young, lively, very friendly and especially enjoyable on the terrace overlooking the cathedral on a summer's evening. Good food also available.

Sampler 17 Nun St. Slightly twee daytime coffee shop – delicious clotted-cream teas, though.

Newport

An ancient and proud little town located a few miles east of Fishguard, **NEWPORT** (Trefdraeth) is set on a gentle slope that courses down to the estuary of the Afon Nyfer. From the main Bridge Street, lanes run down to the river where walks follow **Parrog**, Newport's nearest beach, and the vast dune-backed **Traethmawr**, on the other side of the estuary. In town lie **Carreg Coetan Arthur**, a well-preserved capped burial chamber, and the town's intriguing **castle** (no public access), a modern residence fashioned out of the medieval ruins.

Follow Mill Lane, on the western flank of the castle for the relatively easy two-hour ascent of **Carn Ingli** (Hill of Angels), which to many people is one of Wales's holiest mountains. Bronze-Age hut circles on the top prove that this was a sizeable community even before Iron-Age stone embankments were built. The hill's name comes from the belief that St Brynach lived here in quiet contemplation, with angels as his companions.

Eating options are plentiful in Newport. Solid pub classics, including good curries, are served at the *Royal Oak* on West Street, with pancakes, waffles and crêpes at the daytime *Café Fleur* on Market Street. There's superb, if expensive, local cooking at *Cnapan Country House* on East Street (☎01239/820575; closed Mon throughout year & Tues, Easter–Oct); in summer, they do cheaper barbecue fare out back.

Nevern and Pentre Ifan

Little more than a mile by road east of Newport – but about double that along the pleasant riverside walk – is the straggling village of **NEVERN**, loomed over by a ruined castle. The village's brooding church of St Brynach boasts an intact Norman tower, an inscribed tenth-century Celtic Great Cross standing 13ft high and a darkly atmospheric churchyard roofed by ancient yews. Lanes south of the village lead to the well-signposted cromlech at **Pentre Ifan**, a vast burial stone – the largest in Wales – that dates back over four thousand years. The views from here, on the cusp of the stark Mynydd Preseli hills, are superb.

Central Wales

Central Wales is often viewed as little more than a corridor by which to reach the coast, but look a little closer and it actually has a lot to offer. In the south, the **Brecon Beacons National Park** stretches from the gentle English borderlands in the east to embrace the tourist towns of **Brecon** and **Abergavenny**, the upland range known as the Black Mountain and the immense **Dan-yr-Ogof Showcaves**. To the northeast lie the lonely **Black Mountains** – not to be confused with their singular namesake – and the crumbling remains of **Llanthony Priory**. At the northern corner of the national park, the border town of **Hay-on-Wye** draws in thousands to browse the town's dozens of bookshops.

Crossed by spectacular mountain roads, the sparsely populated countryside to the north of the Beacons is supremely beautiful, dotted with ancient churches and introspective villages. **Llanwrtyd Wells** is the prettiest of Mid-Wales's spa towns, while nearby **Rhayader** is a good base for the grandiose reservoirs of the **Elan Valley**.

Brecon Beacons National Park

The **Brecon Beacons** has the lowest profile of Wales's three national parks, but remains a beguiling destination for thou-

- 0 ━━━━━━━━ 10 miles
- ▲ *Snowdon*
- • Betws-y-Coed
- • Ruthin
- **Wrexham**
- • Llangollen
- *The Maelor*
- *SNOWDONIA NATIONAL PARK*
- • Bala
- *Llyn Tegid*
- *Pistyll Rhaeadr*
- • Harlech
- • Dolgellau
- *Cadair Idris* ▲
- • Welshpool
- **Shrewsbury**
- • Machynlleth
- **ENGLAND**
- • Aberystwyth
- • Ludlow
- Devil's Bridge
- N
- • Rhayader
- • Llandrindod Wells
- ✦ **Dolaucothi**
- • Llanwrtyd Wells
- • Hay-on-Wye
- **Hereford**
- • Brecon
- *BLACK MOUNTAINS*
- *Black Mountain* ▲
- ▲ *Pen-y-Fan*
- *BRECON BEACONS NATIONAL PARK*
- ◉ Dan-yr-Ogof
- • Ystradfellte
- • Abergavenny
- • Monmouth
- • Blaenafon
- • Merthyr Tydfil

sands of walkers. Rounded, spongy hills of grass and rock tumble and climb around river valleys that lie between sandstone and limestone uplands peppered with lakes and villages.

The western Beacons

The most remote parts of the park are to the west, where the vast, open terrain of the **Black Mountain** forms miles of tufted moorland and bleak peaks, tumbling down to the limestone country in the southwestern section – a rocky terrain of rivers, deep caves and spluttering waterfalls. The area provides the most challenging and exhilarating walking in South Wales.

Fforest Fawr (Great Forest), covering a vast expanse of hilly landscape between the Black Mountain and the central Beacons southwest of Brecon, seems something of a misnomer for an area of largely unforested sandstone hills. The hamlet of **YSTRADFELLTE**, little more than a handful of houses, a church and a pub – the *New Inn*, serving basic meals – is a phenomenally popular centre for walking. The Ystradfellte district is recognized as one of the most impressive classic limestone landscapes in the British Isles.

Six miles of upland forest and squelchy moor lie between Ystradfellte and the **Dan-yr-Ogof Showcaves** (April–Oct daily 10am–4pm; last entry 1hr before closing; later admission in July & Aug – call for details ☎01639/730801, ⓦwww.showcaves.co.uk; £10), to the west, which were discovered only in 1912. There are no guided tours: you simply follow the concrete path through a series of caves listening to commentary from unseen speakers. The **Dan-yr-Ogof** cave, the longest in Britain, is followed by the **Cathedral Cave**, a much broader affair winding through a succession of spookily lit caverns where water cascades relentlessly down the walls. **Bone Cave**, the third and final cavern, was known to be inhabited by prehistoric tribes – hence the fenced-off assortment of dressed-up mannequins.

A few yards down a side road opposite the caves, the *Gwyn Arms* serves decent pub **meals**.

The central Beacons

The **central Brecon Beacons** are far more popular for walking and pony trekking than the wet and wild Black Mountain and Fforest Fawr. The terrain here is dramatic, with sweeping peaks rising up out of glacial scoops of land, and at just six miles from the sturdy country seat of Brecon, the mountains are easily accessible too.

The highest peak in the Beacons, **Pen y Fan** (2907ft), together with **Corn Du** (2863ft), half a mile to the west, represent the most popular ascents in the park. The most direct route up is the well-trampled red mud path that starts from Pont ar Daf, half a mile south of Storey Arms on the A470 between Brecon and Merthyr Tydfil. It's a comparatively easy five-mile round trip, gradually climbing up the southern flank of the two peaks.

△ Brecon Beacons

Brecon

The handsome Georgian town of **BRECON** (Aberhonddu), at the northern edge of the Beacons, is a lively place, mainly used as a base to explore the well-waymarked hills to the south, in particular Pen y Fan (see over).

A few sights in town merit a visit. At the junction of The Bulwark and Glamorgan Street, the highlights of the **Brecknock Museum** (Tues–Fri 10am–5pm, Sat 10am–1pm & 2–5pm; April–Sept also Sun noon–5pm; £1) include a walk-through history of Wales and a nineteenth-century assize court, preserved in all its ponderous splendour. To the east, a series of small streets run down from The Watton to the **Monmouth and Brecon Canal**, where you can pick up an afternoon cruise aboard the *Dragonfly* (℡07831/685222; 2hr; £6.50).

North and west of The Bulwark is a cluttered grid of streets, packed with Georgian and Victorian buildings, many of them now fine shops. The High Street Inferior is the main route northwest, passing the **Sarah Siddons** pub, converted from the 1755 birthplace of the famous actress.

At the pub crossroads, Ship Street heads on down to the River Usk, at its confluence with the Honddu, while High Street Superior turns north, past the long **Market Hall** to Priory Hill, which climbs left (west) up to the stark grey buildings of the monastery settlement, centred on the **cathedral**. The building's dumpy external appearance belies its lofty interior, graced with a few intact Norman features.

The Taff Trail

The Taff Trail is a 55-mile route from Brecon to Cardiff Bay that passes through a wonderful cross-section of South Wales scenery: valleys, highland and urban parks. Most of the route – which is not steep, and open to walkers and cyclists – is on forest trails, pathways and country lanes, with pubs and rest areas en route. Everything, including train stations, is marked on the free *Taff Trail* fold-out map, available from tourist offices. ⓦwww.tafftrail.org.uk

Brecon: food and drink

Boars Head Ship St. Two very different bars: the front is simple and sociable, the back is loud and looks like a youth club.

Bull's Head 86 The Struet. Small and cheery locals' pub, with views over the Honddu River and towards the cathedral. Good-value food (with vegetarian and vegan choices) and occasional live music.

The Café 39 High St. Great daytime café, with a warm, relaxed atmosphere and a good range of coffees and hearty soups and snacks.

Llanfaes Dairy 19 Bridge St. Local dairy for wonderful home-made ice cream, located just across the river.

Tipple & Tiffin Theatr Brycheiniog, Canal Basin. Tapas-style dishes to share, together with a few more substantial options in this airy waterside bistro.

Wellington Hotel The Bulwark. Surprisingly unstuffy hotel bar, a frequent venue for live music, especially jazz.

Abergavenny

With upland scenery on its doorstep, **ABERGAVENNY** (Y Fenni) is an excellent base for forays into the central and eastern sections of the Brecon Beacons. There are only dark, fragmented remains left of Abergavenny's medieval **castle**, whose best features are its serene position near the River Usk, at the bottom of the bowl of surrounding hills, and its **museum** (Mar–Oct daily 11am–1pm & 2–5pm; Nov–Feb Mon–Sat 11am–1pm & 2–4pm Sun 2–5pm; free ⓦwww.abergavenny museum.co.uk). This details the town's history through photographs, billboards and re-created interiors; check out Basil Jones's grocery shop, with stock dating from the 1930s and 1940s.

Abergavenny's parish **church of St Mary**, on Monk Street, contains some superb effigies and tombs that span the entire medieval period. Look too for the **Jesse Tree**, a recumbent, twice-lifesize statue of King David's father, which would once have formed part of an altarpiece tracing the family lineage from Jesse to Jesus.

Abergavenny: food and drink

Great George Cross St. Young and lively pub, especially appealing for good-value snacks, weekend discos and Sunday evening live music.

Greco Cross St. A huge café, great for piles of cheap cholesterol. Open until 7.30pm daily.

Greyhound Vaults Market St. Serves a wide range of tasty, moderately priced Welsh and English specialities, including excellent vegetarian options.

Hen and Chickens 7 Flannel St, off High St. Staunchly traditional pub, with the best beer in town and a regular programme of live music and other events.

Trading Post 14 Neville St. Coffee house and bistro, where you can read the paper over a cappuccino or tuck into £6–10 mains, ranging from tortillas and chicken to tortellini and pizza. Open late until 10pm Thurs–Sat.

The Black Mountains

The northeasternmost section of the Brecon Beacons National Park is known as the **Black Mountains**. It's far quieter than the central belt, with tiny villages, isolated churches and delightful lanes folded into the undulating green landscape. The most popular and rewarding areas for walking are in the east of the mountains.

A few miles into the beautiful Vale of Ewyas, the hamlet of **LLANTHONY** is nothing more than a small cluster of houses, an inn and a few outlying farms around the wide-open ruins of **Llanthony Priory**. Llanthony remains much as it has been for 800 years, retaining a real sense of peace against a backdrop of river and mountain. The priory is believed to have been founded on the site of a ruined chapel around 1100 by Norman knight William de Lacy, who, it is said, was so captivated by the spiritual beauty of the site that he renounced worldly living and founded a hermitage, attracting like-minded recluses and forming Wales' first Augustine priory. The church – with its row of wide, pointed transitional arches and squat tower – and outbuildings still standing today were constructed in the latter half of the twelfth century.

A hundred yards north along the road from the priory is the thick-set *Half Moon Inn*, home of superb beer and good-value **food**.

Hay-on-Wye

The sleepy border town of **HAY-ON-WYE** (Y Gelli), at the northern tip of the Brecon Beacons, is known to most people for one thing: books. Hay saw its first secondhand bookshop open in 1961 and has since become a bibliophile's paradise, with over thirty bookshops – the largest containing around half a million volumes – alongside an increasing number of antique shops and galleries. Hay's creaky little streets and its setting amongst soft mountains maintain a sense of unhurried charm. In the last week of May, all fashionable London literary life decamps here for the **Hay Festival of Literature**, held in venues around the town (ⓦwww.hayfestival.co.uk).

The best place to start is Richard Booth's **Hay Castle Bookshop**, with racks of overspill books under canopied covers outside, together with honesty boxes for payment. Here – or from the tourist office – you can pick up the invaluable *Hay-on-Wye Booksellers & Printsellers* leaflet (free), detailing all of the town's literary concerns. Just beyond the Castle Bookshop is the **castle** itself, a fire-damaged Jacobean mansion built into the walls of a thirteenth-century fortress.

Hay-on-Wye: food and drink

Blue Boar Castle St. Tasteful wood-panelled bar on the corner with Oxford Road. Excellent beer and reasonable summer food.
Granary Broad St. Unpretentious, moderately priced café and bistro, with a wide range of excellent vegetarian and other meals, many made from local produce. Save space for wonderful desserts, ice cream and good espresso.
Old Black Lion Lion St. Beautiful

olde-worlde pub that avoids any hint of kitsch. Superb, award-winning meals in the bar, or more robust fare in the pricier restaurant.

Swan at Hay Hotel Church St. Good downstairs bar, popular for its pool tables and games machines. Bar snacks are hearty and good value.

Xtreme Organix 10b Castle St. Takeaway deli and small sit-in café offering hearty snacks from local farms. Mon–Sat 9am–11pm.

△ Bookshop window, Hay-on-Wye

Llanwrtyd Wells

The gorgeous scenery around the unspoiled spa town of **LLANWRTYD WELLS**, about twenty miles northwest of Brecon, is one of its biggest attractions, and nowhere is this more evident than in the country to the south, where the remote **Crychan Forest** and the doleful mountains of the **Mynydd Eppynt** make up the northern outcrops of the Brecon Beacons. The town itself is friendly and lively, and the *Neuadd Arms* pub in the main square is the base for a wide range of bizarre annual events (see box).

Wholesome, traditional Welsh dishes and snacks are on offer at the marvellous *Drover's Rest* **restaurant** by the river bridge. The *Stonecroft Inn* on Dolecoed Road is a superb **pub** with great food and regular live folk, blues and rock music.

Llanwrtyd Wells events

Llanwrtyd Wells has become known for the array of eccentric events it hosts throughout the year. The most famous are the **Bog Snorkelling** competition (end of Aug) and the **Man Versus Horse Marathon** (early June), but you could also indulge in a **Bike Bog** challenge (cycling two lengths of a bog underwater; early July); a **Real Ale Wobble** (noncompetitive mountain biking, fuelled by free beer at every checkpoint; mid-Nov); **duck racing** (at the town's festival; early Aug); and many more. See @llanwrtyd-wells.powys.org.uk for details.

Rhayader and the Elan Valley

RHAYADER (Rhaeder Gwy, literally "waterfall on the Wye") is an excellent base for exploring the wild, spartan countryside to the west of the town, a hilly patchwork of waterfalls, bogland, bare peaks and the four interlocking reservoirs of the **Elan Valley**.

Three miles north, just off the A470, the lovely **Gilfach Farm nature reserve** (unrestricted access; free) features mead-

△ Mountain biking, Elan Valley Trail

ows, oak forest, moorland and river habitats, which together support a huge variety of wildlife and flora. A restored longhouse barn has been kitted out as a **visitor and exhibition centre** (April–Sept Fri–Mon 10am–5pm; July & Aug daily 10am–5pm; £2), showing live video footage from ten birds' nests around the reserve. To watch red kites feeding, head to **Gigrin Farm** (£3 @www.gigrin.co.uk), off South Road on the outskirts of town, where they are lured daily at 3pm (2pm in winter). Kite numbers in the region were once down to just a couple of breeding pairs, but today kites have become so common here they've started repopulating the rest of the country.

During the day in Rhayader, *Carole's Old Swan* tearooms, at the junction of West and South streets, is the place to go for simple **food**. Evening meals are good at the moderate *Brynafon* restaurant (℡01597/810735), half a mile south on the road to Builth Wells. Despite having a population of less than two thousand, there are twelve **pubs** in Rhayader, most offering reasonable pub food – or you could head over Bridge Street to the hamlet of Llansantffraed Cwmdeuddwr, for the ancient *Triangle Inn*: darts players must stand in a special hole in the floor to avoid spearing the roof, and you have to cross the road to get to its toilets.

Pistyll Rhaeadr

Wales's highest waterfall (at 240ft), **Pistyll Rhaeadr** is an enchanting spot in northern Montgomeryshire. The nearest settlement, **LLANRHAEADR-YM-MOCHNANT** – a small, low-roofed village – lies around 13 miles west of the English border town of Oswestry on the B4580, at the foot of the wild walking country of the southern Berwyn Mountains. From the middle of the village, Waterfall Street becomes a lane that heads northwest for four miles to a dead end at the falls. The river tumbles magnificently down a crag in two stages, flowing under a natural stone arch known as the Fairy Bridge; don't miss out on walking to the top of the falls, for vertiginous views down the valley. Staff at the riverside *Tan-y-Pistyll* café can fill you in on the many local legends, and offer food, B&B and camping.

△ Pistyll Rhaeadr

The Cambrian Coast

Wales's western shoreline along Cardigan Bay is known as the Cambrian Coast, a grand mountain-backed sweep of beaches and rocky headlands periodically split by tumbling rivers. Heading north from Cardigan, the coast breaks at some popular seaside resorts before the tiny Georgian harbour town of **Aberaeron**. The coastal and inland routes connect at the cosmopolitan "capital" of Mid-Wales, **Aberystwyth**, from where a narrow-gauge railway climbs out to the popular tourist honeypot of **Devil's Bridge**. Further north, just outside **Machynlleth**, the **Centre for Alternative Technology** is Britain's most impressive showpiece for sustainable living. The main road continues due north from Machynlleth, but trains and the smaller coast road skirt west around **Cadair Idris**, a monumental mountain that dominates the southern third of the Snowdonia National Park. Cadair Idris's northern flank slopes down to the market town of **Dolgellau**, while the coastal strip continues to **Harlech** and its impressive castle.

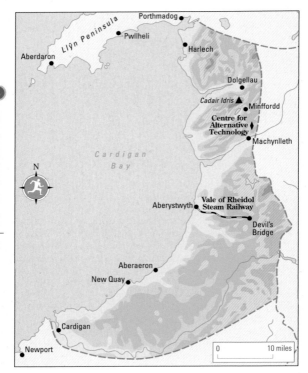

Aberaeron

The primly ordered town of **ABERAERON** is quite unlike anywhere else on this coast. Its large harbour is encircled by brightly painted Georgian houses built in one fell swoop during the early nineteenth century – reputedly from a design by

John Nash. Though Aberaeron's **beach** is unappealing, it's fun just to amble around the waterfront, grazing in the cafés and pubs. Off the main road at the southern end of town, a cluster of ageing stone buildings house **Clôs Pengarreg** (summer daily 10am–6pm; rest of year Mon–Fri 10am–4pm), a better-than-average collection of craft shops.

Aberaeron's essential sight lies three miles east at **Llaner-chaeron**, the substantially restored remains of a late eight-eenth-century Welsh country estate (April–Oct Wed–Sun & bank hols 11.30am–4.30pm, Aug also Tues same hours; £6.40). The original, mostly Edwardian furnishing and fittings are in place, along with an eclectic collection of small antiques. On site also are a working organic farm and two restored walled gardens.

Far and away the best place to **eat** in Aberaeron is the relaxed café/bistro at the *Harbourmaster Hotel* on Pen Cei (☎01545/570755; closed Mon lunch), with delicious lunches and imaginative evening dishes (mains £13–18); it doubles as a convivial bar. Daytime alternatives include *The Hive on the Quay*, Cadwgan Place (☎01545/570445; closed mid-Sept to April), which serves fine local seafood and fabulous **honey ice cream** to eat in or take away. For **drinking**, there's the

Dolphin spotting

Seven miles down the coast from Aberaeron, the atmospheric lit-tle town of New Quay serves as the base for spotting one of only two pods of bottlenose dolphins in Britain: they can sometimes even be seen frolicking by the harbour wall. Plenty of boat trips head out to view them at close quarters; great trips are bookable at New Quay's harbourside Cardigan Bay Marine Wildlife Centre (April–Oct daily 10am–5pm; ☎01545/560032, ⓦwww.cbmwc.org) – their "Dolphin Survey Boat" *Sulaire* (£16 for 2hr, £30 for 4hr, £48 for 8hr) goes well offshore on regular data-gathering exercises, with a ranger on board. Cheaper, shorter trips aboard a rigid-hull inflatable can be had from the New Quay Boat Company (☎07989/175124) at the pier.

△ Aberaeron

Monachty Arms, 7 Market St, with its harbourside beer garden, and the *Black Lion*, Alban Square, which has a good range of guest real ales.

Aberystwyth

One of the liveliest seaside resorts in Wales, **ABERYSTWYTH** is an essential stop along the coast. On a warm summer afternoon there's nothing better than a stroll along the spruced-up Promenade. At its northern end, you can take the clanking 1896 **cliff railway** (daily: July & Aug 10am–6pm; mid-March to June, Sept & Oct 10am–5pm; £2.75 return) up to the summit of the 430-foot **Constitution Hill** (Y Graig Glais). From the bottom of the hill, the Promenade continues round to a rocky headland, where the thirteenth-century **castle** ruins (unrestricted access) stare out to sea. South of the castle is the quieter, sandy **beach** along South Marine Terrace, which peters out by the wide harbour.

Inland from the Promenade, the **National Library of Wales** (Mon–Fri 9.30am–6pm, Sat 9.30am–5pm; free; ⓦwww.llgc .org.uk) is an essential and enjoyable stop for anyone with an interest in matters Welsh, while the nearby **Aberystwyth Arts Centre** is a pleasant place to while away an hour or two, taking in the temporary art exhibitions, catching a movie or enjoying a drink in the café, which affords sublime views over the bay.

Aberystwyth: food and drink

Caffi Blue Creek St James Square. Relaxed little daytime café with comfy sofas and cheerful vibe.

Castle Hotel 37 South Rd. Pub built in the style of an ornate Victorian gin palace. Live local bands at weekends and a good bar menu with vegetarian options.

Lounge 31 Pier St. Student-oriented bar-cum-bistro with decent atmosphere and a dependable menu of good-value steaks, burgers, salads and bruschette. Closed Sun & Mon.

Rummers Bridge St, by the River Rheidol bridge. Late-opening pub and wine bar with sawdust on the floor, outside seating by the river and live music Thurs–Sun.

Ultra Comida 3 Bridge St. Small, classy deli specializing in cheese, olives, tortillas, stuffed baguettes, smoothies and very good coffee, all to take away or consume downstairs where there's a sofa, music and newspapers.

Y Cwps (Coopers Arms) Northgate St. Firmly Welsh local; fun and friendly, with regular folk and jazz nights, plus jam sessions.

Devil's Bridge

Immediately inland from Aberystwyth is the **Vale of Rheidol**, a region of forested glades and remote villages, easily accessed from town by the narrow-gauge steam-hauled **Vale** of **Rheidol Steam Railway** (April–Oct 2–4 services daily; £13 return ⓦwww.rheidolrailway.co.uk). The line terminates at **DEVIL'S BRIDGE** (Pontarfynach), a tiny settlement twelve miles east of Aberystwyth.

The main attraction here is the remarkable bridge itself, where three roads converge and cross the churning River Mynach yards above its confluence with the Rheidol to form three bridges, one on top of the other. The road bridge in front of the *Hafod Hotel* is the most modern of the three, dating from 1901. Immediately below it is the stone bridge from 1753, and, at the bottom, the original bridge, dating from the eleventh century. To see the bridges – and it's well worth it – you have to enter the turnstiles (£1) on either side of the modern road bridge.

On the opposite side of the road is a ticket office (Easter–Oct daily 9.45am–5pm) – pay £2.50 or pass through turnstiles (£2) when closed – which opens out onto a path leading down into the valley and ultimately to the crashing **Mynach Falls**.

Machynlleth

Shortlisted for Welsh capital in the 1950s, handsome **MACH-YNLLETH** (pronounced *mah-hun-cthleth*) was the site of Owain Glyndŵr's embryonic fifteenth-century Welsh parliament. His modest black-and-white-fronted **Parliament House** (Easter–Sept Mon–Sat 10am–5pm; free) sits halfway along Heol Maengwyn. Displays chart the course of Glyndŵr's life and the 1404 parliament, when he controlled almost all of what we now know as Wales. Opposite the Parliament House are the landscaped grounds of **Plas Machynlleth**, the elegant seventeenth-century mansion of the Marquess of Londonderry.

Up Penrallt Street, the **Museum of Modern Art, Wales** (MOMA Cymru; Mon–Sat 10am–4pm; free) hosts an ongoing programme of temporary exhibitions. To see local work in a more commercial setting, don't miss the superb **Spectrum**

Gallery (Mon–Sat 10am–5pm), a UK leader in ceramics, housed in a beautiful blue-fronted building on the main street.

There are plenty of **cafés, restaurants and pubs** in town, including the popular veggie wholefood *Quarry Café*, near the clocktower on Heol Maengwyn; for good-value carnivorous fare, try the *Caffi Maengwyn* along the street by the Spar supermarket. Lunch and dinner are great at the *Wynnstay Arms*, which also has a pizzeria in its courtyard bar. The liveliest pub in town is the *Skinners Arms* on Heol Penrallt, run a close second by the *White Lion*, by the clocktower.

Centre for Alternative Technology

Since its foundation in the middle of the oil crisis of 1974, the **Centre for Alternative Technology (CAT)** or *Canolfan y Dechnoleg Amgen* (daily: Aug 9.30am–6pm; Easter–July, Sept & Oct 10am–5.30pm; Nov–Easter 10am–dusk; £8, less if you

△ Centre for Alternative Technology

Walking on Cadair Idris

To the north of Machynlleth, the southern coastal reaches of Snowdonia National Park are almost entirely dominated by **Cadair Idris** (2930ft), a five-peaked massif. Tennyson claimed never to have seen "anything more awful than the great veil of rain drawn straight over Cader Idris", but catch it on a good day, and the views from the top – occasionally stretching as far as Ireland – are stunning.

The steepest and most dramatic ascent follows the **Minffordd Path** (6 miles; 5hr round trip; 2900ft ascent), a justifiably popular route that starts from the tiny hamlet of **MINFFORDD** in the Talyllyn Valley, a short way north of Machynlleth. The route makes a full circuit around the rim of **Cwm Cau**, probably the country's most dramatic mountain cirque. Walkers can refresh themselves afterwards in the **Minffordd Hotel**, a seventeenth-century farmhouse and drovers' inn that serves both bar **meals** and pricey four-course dinners.

Further information on walking in Wales is available from ⓦwww .walking.visitwales.com and ⓦwww.ramblers.org.uk/wales.

arrive by bike or public transport; ☎01654/705950, ⓦwww. cat.org.uk), three miles north of Machynlleth off the A487, has become one of the biggest attractions in Wales. Over that time, seven acres of a once-derelict slate quarry have been turned into an almost entirely sustainable community, generating eighty percent of its own power from wind, sun and water.

But this is no back-to-the-land hippie commune. Right from the start, the idea was to embrace technology – much of the on-site equipment was developed and built here, reflecting the centre's achievements in this field – and, most importantly, to promote its application in urban situations.

CAT's earnest education is leavened with flashes of pizzazz, particularly in the water-balanced **cliff railway** (Easter–Oct only), which whisks the visitor 200ft up to the main site from the car park. It's also a beautiful site, sensitively landscaped using local slate and wood; you could easily spend half a day exploring. The wholefood **restaurant** turns out delicious food.

Dolgellau

DOLGELLAU (pronounced *dol-gethl-aye*) is the most convenient access point to the southern reaches of the Snowdonia National Park. As well as offering some wonderful walks, including a strenuous hike up Cadair Idris, Dolgellau offers plenty of evening diversions in the form of good pubs and restaurants and a fair bit of live music. This comes to a head during the annual **Sesiwn Fawr** (literally "Big Session"; ⓦwww.sesiwnfawr.co.uk), a long weekend of bands and musical shenanigans that takes place in mid-July in pubs and on open-air stages all over town.

Dolgellau: food and drink

Aber Cottage Tea Room Smithfield St. One of the nicest cafés in town.
Stag Inn Bridge St. Straightforward town-centre pub with good beer and a garden.

Y Sospan Queen's Square ☎01341/423174. Dependable café-bistro behind the tourist office, serving coffee, decent daytime meals and dinners (booking necessary), all at modest prices.

Harlech

One of the highlights of the Cambrian coast is charming **HARLECH**, 21 miles by road northwest of Dolgellau. Its time-worn castle alone is worth a visit, and the town behind commands one of Wales's finest views – over the Morfa Harlech dunes across Cardigan Bay, and north to the jagged peaks of Snowdonia. Harlech is also blessed with some of the coast's best **beaches**.

Construction of the spectacular **castle** (April, May & Oct daily 9.30am–5pm; June–Sept daily 9.30am–6pm; Nov–March Mon–Sat 9.30am–4pm, Sun 11am–4pm; £3.50), squatting on its 200-foot bluff, began in 1283. Much of the outermost ring has been destroyed, leaving only the twelve-foot-thick curtain walls rising up 40ft to the exposed battlements, and only the towering gatehouse prevents you walking the full circuit.

Harlech: food and drink

Cemlyn High St ☎01766/780425. By day, an upscale café serving fine loose-leaf teas and gourmet coffees, by night a quality (though mid-priced) restaurant for which booking is advised.

Lion Hotel Pen Dref, just up from the central crossroads. About the liveliest pub in Harlech, with hand-pumped ales and good home-cooked bar meals.

Plâs Café High St ☎01766/780204. Unpretentious café-restaurant with well-prepared lunches and afternoon teas served in a glass-fronted dining room or on a garden terrace with sensational views. Also open for mid-priced dinners. Closed Jan.

△ Harlech Castle

5

Snowdonia and the Llŷn

Snowdonia is North Wales's crowning glory, a tightly packed bundle of soaring cliff faces, jagged peaks and plunging waterfalls. The **Snowdonia National Park** is home to Wales's highest mountain, **Snowdon** (Eryri), where winter snows cling to 3000-foot peaks well into April. Small settlements are dotted in the valleys here, making great

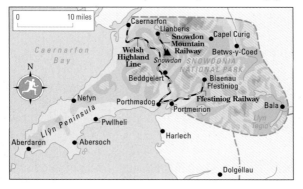

bases or places to rest, chief among them **Betws-y-Coed**. Others, like **Beddgelert**, **Llanberis** and **Blaenau Ffestiniog** are former mining or quarry towns still brimming with interest.

West of Snowdonia, the mountain landscape bleeds into the softer contours of the **Llŷn** Peninsula, which juts into the Irish Sea. Linked to Snowdonia by the magnificent, narrow-gauge **Ffestiniog Railway**, its first settlement is the harbour town of **Porthmadog**, best-known for its proximity to the Italianate dream village of **Portmeirion**. Wales ends in a flourish of small coves around **Aberdaron**. Finally, roads loop back along the Llŷn, via **Nant Gwrtheyrn** to the tip of the north coast where **Caernarfon**, the heart of this nationalist, Welsh-speaking area, is overshadowed by its mighty castle.

Snowdon

The highest British mountain south of the Scottish Grampians, the **Snowdon** massif (3650ft) forms a star of shattered ridges with three major peaks – Crib Goch, Crib-y-ddysgl and Y Lliwedd – and the summit, **Yr Wyddfa**, crowning the lot.

△ View from Snowdon summit

Rock climbing

Wales offers some of Britain's best **rock climbing**. In the south of the country, the pick of the crags are the sea cliffs of Gower and the Pembrokeshire Coast, but the vast majority of climbing destinations lie to the north in **Snowdonia**. A predominance of low-lying crags combined with easy accessibility mean that on any sunny weekend you'll spot brightly coloured figures hanging from almost every cliff face. The principal areas to head for are the Llanberis Pass, Ogwen Valley and Tremadog (near Porthmadog). The best general guide for experienced climbers is *Rock Climbing in Snowdonia* by Paul Williams, stocked in the region's climbing shops.

Beginners should contact Plas y Brenin: The National Mountain Centre, near Capel Curig (℡01690/720214, ⓦwww.pyb.co.uk), or the British Mountaineering Council (℡0161/445 6111, ⓦwww.thebmc.co.uk), which can put you in touch with climbing guides and people running courses.

Snowdon sports some of the finest walking and scrambling in the park. Winter is the longest season for ice climbers and cramponed walkers.

There is no longer a tumulus on the top of Snowdon, but the Welsh term Yr Wyddfa means "The Burial Place" – suggesting that people have been climbing the mountain for millennia. The **Llanberis Path** remains one of the most popular routes up, though many prefer the three shorter and steeper alternatives from the Pen-y-Pass car park at the top of the Llanberis Pass. By far the most dramatic route is the **Snowdon Horseshoe**, which calls at all four of the high peaks.

Llanberis

Hikers exploring Snowdon's northern flank mostly base themselves at **LLANBERIS**, a former slate-mining town on the shores of Llyn Padarn near the picturesque ruins of the thirteenth-century **Dolbadarn Castle** (unrestricted access). The former slate quarries which carved away the hills to the north of town are the setting for the **National Slate Museum** (Easter–Oct daily 10am–5pm; Nov–Easter daily except Sat 10am–4pm; free ⓦwww.museumwales.ac.uk) where former quarry workers demonstrate their skills at turning an inch-thick slab into six, or even eight, perfectly smooth slivers.

The rack-and-pinion **Snowdon Mountain Railway** (mid-March to Oct 9am–5pm; ☎0870/458 0033 ⓦwww.snowdon-railway.co.uk) chugs its way from Llanberis up the mountain, often pushed by a feisty little steam loco offering spectacular views over Pen-y-Pass to the village of Nant Peris.

There are several good places to fortify yourself in Llanberis, including *Pete's Eats*, 40 High St, which serves up large portions of top-value caff food and a few, more delicate dishes.

Pen-y-Pass

Five miles east of Llanberis is the lofty saddle of **PEN-Y-PASS**, the deepest, narrowest and craggiest of Snowdon's passes. At its head is a hostel, café and car park, trailhead for several of the finest walking routes up the mountain. A mile further east is the nearest **pub**, the atmospheric *Pen-y-Gwryd*. The first party to climb Everest in the 1950s were based here for winter training; they left many mementoes and even brought back a chunk of Everest itself, now enjoying pride of place in the bar.

Capel Curig

There's scarcely a building in tiny **CAPEL CURIG**, five miles east of Pen-y-Pass, that isn't of some use to hikers, whether as accommodation, a shop selling mountain gear or somewhere to refuel the body. **Plas-y-Brenin: The National Mountain Centre** (ⓦwww.pyb.co.uk), just outside the village centre, is the main draw, with information, courses, a climbing wall, dry ski-slope and all kinds of other activities.

Betws-y-Coed

Six miles east of Capel Curig, **BETWS-Y-COED** (pronounced *betoos-er-coyd*) has an undeniably appealing setting, overlooked by the conifer-clad slopes of the Gwydyr Forest Park. None of the serious mountain walks start from here, although the town is a major centre for **mountain biking** in the forest: the trail scenery is fantastic, particularly along the higher sections. Several places in town rent mountain bikes, starting from around £20 a day.

Beddgelert and around

Almost all of the vast quantity of rain that falls on Snowdon spills down into the Glaslyn River in Nantgwynant or the Colwyn River in Nant Colwyn. At the rivers' confluence – amidst majestic mountain scenery – huddle the few dozen hard grey houses that make up **BEDDGELERT**. It's a curiously enchanting place, with front gardens and window boxes bursting with flowers, and lots of places to eat and drink.

A sixteenth-century former farmhouse, inn, general store and tearooms right in the heart of the village – known as Llywelyn Cottage – is now **Tŷ Isaf** (Easter–Oct Wed–Sun 1–4pm; free Ⓦwww.nationaltrust.org.uk), which puts on good exhibitions usually on some aspect of Snowdonia's cultural history. The red-brown stain on the hillside opposite identifies the **Sygun Copper Mine** (Easter–Oct daily 9.30am–5pm; £7.95 Ⓦwww.sygun coppermine.co.uk), whose ore drew first the Romans, then nineteenth-century prospectors. A 45-minute self-guided tour leads through the multiple levels of tunnels and galleries, accompanied by the disembodied voice of a miner describing his working life.

Beddgelert: food and drink

Beddgelert Bistro & Antiques On the north side of the river bridge

☏01766/890543. Scones with clotted cream by day; wild goose

breast in triple sec, Anglesey lobster or leek and mushroom pie (£11–19) by night. Book ahead for dinner.
Glaslyn On the south side of the river bridge. Great ice-cream shop with dozens of flavours for takeaway and a family-style restaurant tucked in behind.
River Garden Restaurant ℡01766/890551. Centrally located with a waterside terrace serving hearty breakfasts, mid-priced meals and cream teas. Worth booking.

Blaenau Ffestiniog

Deep in a stark grey fold at the head of the Vale of Ffestiniog hunkers **BLAENAU FFESTINIOG**, a forbidding but oddly attractive place. Slate mining still continues here, and you can get a sense of what a miner's life used to be like at the **Llechwedd Slate Caverns** (daily: March–Sept 10am–6pm; Oct–Feb 10am–5pm; single tour £9.25, both tours £14.75; ⓦwww.llechwedd-slate-caverns.co.uk), where the Miners' Underground Tramway takes you along a third of a mile of level track to an enormous cavern hewn out of the rock. On the wilder Deep Mine Tour you descend on Britain's steepest-inclined railway for a self-guided tour that concentrates on the social life of miners. The splendid **Ffestiniog Railway** (see below) links the town with Porthmadog.

Porthmadog

The bustling town of **PORTHMADOG** was once the busiest slate port in North Wales, and is now a pleasant base for visiting the Italianate folly of Portmeirion, three miles to the east, and travelling on the wonderful **Ffestiniog Railway** (April–Oct 4–8 services daily; Nov–March services several days a week; £16.95 return; ℡01766/516024, ⓦwww.festrail

Watersports at Bala

Approximately 20 miles west of Blaenau Ffestiniog, the little town of **BALA** (Y Bala) lies at the northern end of Wales' largest natural lake, **Llyn Tegid** (Bala Lake), and is a major water-sports centre. The four-mile-long body of water is perfect for **windsurfing**. Down on the shores of the lake, Bala Adventure and Watersports Centre (℡01678/521059, ⓦwww.balawatersports.com) runs courses in windsurfing, open-water kayaking and sailing; individual instruction costs around £35 for half a day.

Kayak and whitewater rafting fans can make for the National White Water Centre at **Canolfan Tryweryn** (℡01678/521083, ⓦwww.ukwhitewater.co.uk), four miles west. When water is released – typically around 200 days a year – it crashes down a mile and a half through the slalom site where frequent competitions take place on summer weekends. Go for two runs down (60–70min; £28), a two-hour session (4–7 people from £228), or, stepping up a notch, try the Orca, a two-person inflatable in which you tackle the rapids unguided (half-day £70 per person). Proficient **kayakers** can also take to the water (£7 per day for Canoeing Association members, £14 others). Gear rental is available.

.co.uk), which originally carried down slates from Blaenau Ffestiniog. The waterfront is the most interesting place to wander, not least because the last surviving slate shed contains the **Maritime Museum** (Easter & June–Sept daily 11am–5pm; £1 ℡01766 513736), a modest collection of ships in glass cases, with panels telling of the town's shipbuilding role and its importance in carrying slate around the world.

Porthmadog: food and drink

Allport's Corner of Snowdon and Madoc streets. Ordinary-looking fish-and-chip shop that is frequently honoured as the best in the region, or even in Wales. **Caffi y Morwr Madog** Pencei. Small,

modern café serving decent coffee and a range of bagels, croissants and desserts, as well as "Catch of the Day" meals. **Eric Jones' Café** Prenteg. Go a mile north of Porthmadog to Tre-

madog, then a mile east on the A498. Good, solid food wolfed down by climbers of the nearby Tremadog crags. There's a useful notice board and a small stock of climbing gear and guidebooks for sale. Usually open to 6pm, later on summer weekends.
Passage to India Tandoori 26a

Lombard St ☎01766/512144. Typical curry-restaurant menu disguises the fact that this is one of the best such places around. Most dishes are £6–8 and there's a good selection of chef's specials.
Y Llong (The Ship) 14 Lombard St. Lively pub selling good real ales.

Portmeirion

The unique, privately-owned Italianate village of **PORT-MEIRION** (daily 9.30am–5.30pm; ⓦwww.portmeirion-village.com; £6.80) is set on a small rocky peninsula in Tremadog Bay, three miles east of Porthmadog, near Minffordd. Perhaps best known as "The Village" in the 1960s British cult TV series *The Prisoner*, Portmeirion was the brainchild of eccentric architect **Clough Williams-Ellis**. His dream was to build an ideal village to enhance rather than blend in with its surroundings, using a "gay, light-opera sort of approach". The result certainly

△ Portmeirion

is theatrical: a stage set with a lucky dip of unwanted buildings arranged to distort perspectives and reveal tantalizing glimpses of the sea or the expansive sands behind.

The Llŷn

Travelling west of Porthmadog, past the battle-worn castle above **Cricieth**, you move onto the Llŷn Peninsula. If you're here on a Wednesday, drop into the market in modest **Pwllheli**; otherwise, head out beyond **Abersoch** – scene of the excellent **Wakestock festival** (see box) – and on through undulating pasture to the small lime-washed fishing village of **ABERDARON**, two miles short of the tip of the peninsula. Here you really feel you're approaching the end of Wales. Now just a few dozen houses, this peaceful village was once the last stop on a pilgrim trail to Ynys Enlli or Bardsey Island, around the headland. Just back from the water, the fourteenth-century stone *Y Gegin Fawr* (The Big Kitchen) served as the pilgrims' final gathering place before the treacherous crossing, and now operates as a café. The twelfth-century **Church of St Hywyn** (daily: April–Oct 10am–5pm; Nov–March 10am–4pm; free @www.st-hywyn.org.uk), on the cliffs behind the stony beach, was ministered by Wales's greatest modern poet, R.S. Thomas, until he retired in 1978. Displays on Thomas have pride of place in the twin-naved interior, beside a pair of Latin-inscribed fifth-century gravestones.

Wakestock

Attracting some twenty thousand punters every July, Abersoch's **Wakestock festival** (@www.wakestock.co.uk) mixes wakeboarding contests and surfing on the beaches of the Llŷn with BMX-riding, cutting-edge music acts and DJs. It has rapidly become a magnet for bleach-haired beauties of both sexes from all over Europe – proof of just how far Wales's water-sports scene has come on in recent years.

The north Llŷn coast

Sprinkled with small coves and sweeping beaches between rocky bluffs, the **north Llŷn coast** makes a dramatic contrast with the busier south, and is ideal cycling territory. **PORTH DINLLAEN**, a mile west of Nefyn, is a shoreline hamlet looking out onto a pristine, sweeping bay; the *Tŷ Coch Inn* here (closed Sun eve ☎01758 720498 ⓦwww.tycoch.co.uk) is the most idyllic spot for a beer you could imagine.

Northeast of Nefyn the mountains of Yr Eifl rise steeply then plummet into the sea to the north. A fold in the mountains is called **Nant Gwrtheyrn** (Vortigern's Valley) because it's supposed to be the final resting place of the Celtic chieftain Vortigern. The ancient Welsh language is kept alive and taught at the impressive **Nant Gwrtheyrn Welsh Language and Heritage Centre** (ⓦwww.nantgwr.com), in the rows of converted granite quarry cottages at the foot of the valley.

Caernarfon Castle

In 1283, Edward I started work on **Caernarfon Castle** (April, May & Oct daily 9.30am–5pm; June–Sept daily 9.30am–6pm; Nov–March Mon–Sat 9.30am–4pm, Sun 11am–4pm; £4.90 ⓦwww.cadw.wales.gov.uk), the strongest link in his Iron Ring and the decisive hammer-blow to any Welsh aspirations of autonomy. The Welsh had long associated their town with the eastern capital of the Roman Empire: Caernarfon's old name, Caer Cystennin, was also the name used for Constantinople. Edward's architect, James of St George, exploited this connection in the distinctive limestone and sandstone banding and polygonal towers, both reminiscent of the Theodosian walls in present-day Istanbul. As a military monument of its time, the castle is supreme, and it still has a brooding, imperious presence. Seized only once, before it was finished, it then withstood two sieges by Owain Glyndŵr with a complement of only 28 men-at-arms.

The North Coast and Borderlands

Wales's **north coast** and its natural extension, the island of **Anglesey**, encompass both the geographical extremities of the country and the extremes of Welsh life – from brash English-dominated seaside towns to villages as Welsh as they ever were.

Llangollen in the Dee Valley has an international eisteddfod folk music festival each July, and enough ruins, rides and rambles to tempt visitors throughout the rest of the the year. In the northeast of the country sits delightful **Ruthin**, though most people pass up its historic attractions in favour of the coastal resorts. Of these, Victorian **Llandudno**, at the foot of the Great

Orme peninsula, remains a cut above the rest. Nearby **Conwy** boasts an intact ring of walls presided over by a stunning early medieval castle, while the absorbing town of **Beaumaris** on the island of Anglesey features another mighty castle, built to a highly advanced concentric design. West of Anglesey lies **Holy Island**, with its patchwork of rural communities and scattering of Neolithic remains.

Llangollen

In the South East, reached more easily from Wrexham or Oswestry, **LLANGOLLEN** is the embodiment of a Welsh town in both setting and character. It lies clasped tightly in the narrow Dee Valley, between the Berwyn and Eglwyseg mountains. Along the valley's floor, the waters of the River Dee (Afon Dyfrdwy) cut a wide arc around the base of **Castell Dinas Brân**, a conical tor surmounted by the evocative ruins of a native Welsh castle, built in the 1230s. This is a great place to be when the sun is setting, some 800ft above the town. A signposted path heads up from Llangollen Wharf.

Down below, the Dee licks the angled buttresses of Llangollen's weighty Gothic **bridge**, which has spanned the river since the fourteenth century. On its south bank, half a dozen streets, their houses harmoniously straggling up the rugged hillsides, are labelled in both Welsh and English, and form the core of the scattered settlement flung out across the low hills.

Turner came to paint the swollen river and the Cistercian ruin of **Valle Crucis** (daily 10am–5pm; closes earlier in winter; £2.50), a couple of miles up the valley; John Ruskin found the town "entirely lovely in its gentle wildness"; and writer George Borrow made Llangollen his base for the early part of his 1854 tour detailed in *Wild Wales*. The rich and famous came not only for the scenery, but to visit the celebrated **Ladies of Llangollen**, an eccentric pair of lesbians who lived in the town for fifty years after 1780 and became the toast of society from their modest black-and-white timbered house, **Plas Newydd** (Easter–Oct daily 10am–5pm; £3.50). In early July, Llangollen struggles to cope with the thousands of visitors to Wales's celebration of worldwide folk music, the **International Music Eisteddfod**.

Llangollen: food and drink

Bryn Howel Hotel Trevor ☎01978/860331. Formal, expensive, award-winning restaurant with great views of Dinas Brân across the lawns.

Bull Inn Castle St. Lively town pub (with a beer garden) that's the main gathering place for Llangollen's youth.

Corn Mill Dee Lane ☎01978/869555. Superb conversion of a town-centre mill, with outside decking for warm days or evenings. Decent, modern café-bar food is served.

Gales Wine Bar 18 Bridge St ☎01978/860089. Old church pews and one of the most extensive cellars around make this a great place for an evening of wine glugging, with moderately priced bistro-style food to soak it all up.

Hand Hotel 26 Bridge St. Straightforward local pub where you can listen to the male voice choir in full song at 7.30pm on Fri.

Ruthin

Though surrounded by modern housing and known mainly for its livestock market, **RUTHIN** (Rhuthun), built on a commanding rise in the Vale of Clwyd roughly twenty miles north of Llangollen, should not be missed, having some of the finest food and lodgings in the area, and an attractive knot of half-timbered buildings between its church and a red stone **castle**. The most photographed building in town is the **Myddleton Arms pub**, built in 1657 in Dutch style and topped by seven dormer windows known as "The Eyes of Ruthin", which overlook the square.

The recently restored **Ruthin Gaol** (May–Oct daily 10am–5pm; rest of year Sat & Sun same hours; ⓦwww.ruthingaol .co.uk; £3.50) lies five minutes' walk down Clwyd Street from St Peter's Square. Though there was a prison on the site from 1654 to 1916, the so-called "Gruelling Experience" focuses on the Victorian era.

Ruthin's **café and restaurant** scene includes the *Bay Tree Café*, right by the tourist office, which is good for light daytime meals, and the trendier *Manorhaus*, on Well Street, where you can sit out-side. *Ye Olde Cross Keys*, a mile southeast of Ruthin on the B5105, is a welcoming **pub** with excellent, moderately priced meals.

Llandudno

The twin limestone hummocks of the 680-foot Great Orme and its southern cousin the Little Orme provide a dramatic frame for the gently curving Victorian frontage of **LLAN-DUDNO**, on Wales's north coast. The core of the town occu-pies a low isthmus between two beachfronts, West Shore and more developed Llandudno Bay. Despite the arrival of more rumbustious fun-seekers, Llandudno retains an undeniably dignified air. It's also blessed with the best choice of restaurants in North Wales, ranging from budget cafés to some of the most expensive places in the country.

Note that mainline trains stop at **Llandudno Junction**, about four miles south of town, nearer to Conwy; the more central station, on a slower branch line, is called simply Llandudno.

First-time visitors are inevitably drawn to the **pier** (open all year; free) jutting into Llandudno Bay. Once the embodiment of Llandudno's ornate Victoriana, its neat wooden deck is overrun

△ Llandudno, from Great Orme

in summer with kids clamouring to board the modest fairground rides. From the pier, it's a leisurely ten-minute stroll along The Promenade, with its regal four-storey terraced hotels, to Vaughan Street and the region's premier contemporary art gallery, **Oriel Mostyn** (Mon–Sat 10am–5pm; free ⓦwww.mostyn. org). Towards the Orme, the **Llandudno Museum** at 17–19 Gloddaeth St (Easter–Oct Tues–Sat & bank hols 10.30am–1pm & 2–5pm, Sun 2.15–5pm; Nov–Easter Tues–Sat 1.30–4.30pm; £1.50) exhibits items unearthed in local copper mines, plus Roman artefacts and a rural kitchen from Llanberis.

Llandudno: food and drink

Bodysgallen Hall 3 mile south of town on the A470 ☎01492/584466. Top-notch traditional and modern British fare in one of Britain's best country hotels.

Cottage Loaf Market St. Flagstoned pub built from ships' timbers atop an old bake house. Good food at lunchtime, good drinks all day.

Ham Bone Food Hall Lloyd St. Excellent deli offering great takeaway sandwiches to order, along with a range of pies and salads.

Kings Head Old Rd, by the bottom of the tramway. Llandudno's oldest pub, serving substantial bar meals, ranging from Welsh Rarebit to noisettes of lamb.

Seahorse Seafood Bistro and Restaurant 7 Church Walks ☎01492/875315. Intimate dinner-only basement bistro with slate-tiled floor and an intriguing modern British menu that borrows from East Asia. Three courses £25. Closed Sun & Mon.

Conwy

Few towns in Wales pack so much into such a small space as **CONWY**, four miles southwest of Llandudno (and less than a mile west of Llandudno Junction train station). Almost everything of interest is contained within a complete belt of **town walls**, sections of which can be climbed for excellent views over the town, the Conwy estuary and Conwy's domineering castle.
In the centre of this ring stands the early fourteenth-century

timber-and-stone **Aberconwy House** (April–Oct daily except Tues 11am–5pm; £3 ⓦwww.nationaltrust.org.uk), Conwy's sole medieval building, which somehow managed to survive several fires and Victorian improvements. Around the corner, the Elizabethan **Plas Mawr** (Tues–Sun: April, May & Sept 9.30am–5pm; June–Aug 9.30am–6pm; Oct 9.30am–4pm; £4.90, joint ticket with Conwy Castle £7 ⓦwww.cadw.wales. gov.uk) is the town's grandest residence. It was built in Dutch style for Robert Wynn, one of the first native Welsh people allowed to live in the walled town. The tour of the house concludes with a superb exhibition about Tudor and Stuart attitudes to disease and cleanliness, which manages to be compulsively gory, hilarious and highly informative to boot.

Conwy Castle itself (April, May & Oct daily 9.30am–5pm; June–Sept daily 9.30am–6pm; Nov–March Mon–Sat 9.30am–4pm, Sun 11am–4pm; £4.50 ⓦwww.cadw.wales.gov.uk) was built in just five years, after 1283, by Edward I. Overlooked by a low hill, the castle appears less easily defended than others along the coast, but it has eight massive towers in a rectangle around the two wards protected by turrets atop the four eastern towers.

△ Conwy Castle

Strolling along the ramparts you can look down onto a roofless but largely intact interior, with the 130-foot-long Great Hall and the King's Apartments both well preserved. The only part of the castle to have kept its roof is the **Chapel Tower**, named for the small room built into the wall whose semicircular apse still shows some heavily worn carving.

Conwy: food and drink

Archway 12 Bangor Rd. Quality fish-and-chips to eat in or take away, with pizza/pasta options.
Edwards 18 High St. Good deli with a decent salad bar; the place to stock up for picnics.
Groes Inn Tyn-y-Groes, 2 miles south on B5106 to Llanrwst. An atmospheric fifteenth-century pub claiming to be the oldest licensed house in Wales. Excellent bar meals and cask ales.

Liverpool Arms The Quay. Compact pub built into the town wall. Dockside location makes it a perfect spot on warm summer evenings.
Tower Coffee House Castle Square. Great café set in one of the town-wall towers, with estuary views. Come for panini, baguettes, espresso and good cakes.

Beaumaris

Beaumaris, on the island of Anglesey, a few miles over the bridge from Bangor, is dominated by its **castle** (April, May & Oct daily 9.30am–5pm; June–Sept daily 9.30am–6pm; Nov–March Mon–Sat 9.30am–4pm, Sun 11am–4pm; £3.50 ⓦwww.cadw.wales.gov.uk). The most picturesque of Edward I's gargantuan fortresses, it was built in response to Madog ap Llywelyn's capture of Caernarfon in 1294. The architect, James of St George, produced a symmetrical octagonal form, his finest and most highly evolved expression of concentric design. Lacking the domineering majesty of Caernarfon, Conwy or Harlech, its low outer walls seem

6

△ Beaumaris Castle

almost welcoming – belying the deadly ingenuity of its design.

For a small place, Beaumaris has a good selection of **cafés and restaurants**. The *Pier House Café*, Bron Menai, The Front, is a cheerful place with sea views, all-day breakfasts, bagels, grills and daily specials. Beaumaris's top hotel, *Ye Olde Bull's Head Inn*, has a cosy old-fashioned bar, plus a bare-boards brasserie and more formal upstairs restaurant, both serving a contemporary menu. Best **pub** is the *Sailor's Return*, Church Street, known for its excellent bar meals.

Holy Island

Holy Island (Ynys Gybi) – linked by bridges to Anglesey – is blessed with Anglesey's finest scenery. The spectacular sea cliffs around **South Stack**, and the Stone-Age and Roman remains on **Holyhead Mountain** are just a few miles from downbeat **HOLYHEAD** (pronounced *holly-head*), which has excellent transport connections by ferry to Ireland and by high-speed train to London.

Holyhead Mountain and South Stack

The northern half of Holy Island is ranged around the skirts of **Holyhead Mountain** (Mynydd Twˆr), rising 700ft to the west of Holyhead. Its summit is ringed by the remains of the Iron-Age **Caer y Twˆr** (unrestricted access), one of the largest sites in North Wales. A path (45min) leads from the car park at South Stack, two miles west of Holyhead, to the top of Holyhead Mountain, though most people only attempt to walk the few yards from the car park to the clifftop **Ellin's Tower Seabird Centre** (Easter–Sept daily 10am–5.30pm; free). Between April and the end of July, binoculars and closed-circuit TV give an unrivalled opportunity to watch thousands of birds – razorbills, guillemots and the odd puffin – nesting on the nearby sea cliffs.

A twisting path, with over four hundred steps, leads down from the South Stack car park to a suspension bridge over the surging waves, once the keeper's only access to the now fully automated pepper-pot **lighthouse** (Easter–Sept daily 10.30am–5.30pm; £3), built in 1809.

Trearddur Bay and Rhoscolyn

At the pinch of Holy Island's hourglass shape, a couple of miles south of Holyhead, the scattered settlement of **TREARD-DUR BAY** (Bae Trearddur) shambles across low grassy hills, around a deeply indented bay punctuated by rocky coves. There's no centre to speak of, but it's a much nicer base than Holyhead; it even has a good, clean swimming **beach**.

At the southern tip of the island, a mile or so south of Trearddur Bay, a lane runs down to **RHOSCOLYN**, another scattered seaside settlement, even smaller and more appealing. With a couple of exquisite sandy beaches, lots of rocky outcrops and some delightful coastal walking, this is the ideal place to spend a few days chilling out. There's a small range of watersports gear for hire, plus campsite and hostel, at Outdoor Alternative (☎01407/860469, ⊛www.outdooralternative.org), a few yards from the beach.

Green Wales

The unspoiled natural environment of Wales is the primary attraction for forty percent of visitors – not surprising when you consider the diversity of landscapes and experiences on offer. In recent years many organisations and businesses have turned towards more 'green' (sustainable) practices in order to protect this environment. Here are some examples:

Centre for Alternative Technology

Ⓦ www.cat.org.uk, see p.63

This award-winning initiative promotes the use of technology to address issues of environmental concern. Over more than thirty years, the Centre has grown into an almost entirely sustainable community, generating most of its own energy.

Coed Hills

Ⓦ www.coedhills.co.uk

This leading venue for art in the environment features an 80 acre woodland sculpture trail. Visitors also have the opportunity to explore eco lifestyles and learn more about renewable energy.

Cwmni Gwynt Teg Wind Farm

Ⓦ www.ailwynt.co.uk

Owned and operated by a collective of three farming families, Cwmni Gwynt Teg wind farm opened in 2003 in the Conwy

Valley. The first community-owned project of its kind, the farm enjoys overwhelming local support. When the final phase, named Ail Wynt, is completed, the farm's output will match the energy needs of 2500 homes.

Farmers' markets

Ⓦ www.organicwales.com

Wales has around 25–30 farmers' markets – great places to buy locally produced food, find a wide selection of free-range and organic produce and plug into the local community as well. The website above also has listings of organic cafés and restaurants.

Green Accommodation

Ⓦ www.breconbeacons.org.uk; Ⓦ www.tyf.com; Ⓦ www.tipiwest.co.uk

Wales has many pioneering environmentally friendly hotels and lodgings. There are over 30 places to stay in the Brecon Beacons National Park alone, that have achieved the Green Dragon Award - which shows that they are improving their energy efficiency, recycling and water use, as well as working to reduce their impact on the environment. In Pembrokeshire, TYF is the first carbon-neutral outdoor adventure company in the world and includes Wales's first organic hotel – an eighteenth century converted windmill in St Davids, which serves only organic local food and drink. More simple accommodation can be found six miles from Cardigan, where Tipi West can comfortably sleep up to 25 adults in three large tipis, based on a working farm. The tipis are furnished with coconut matting and heated with a central open fire. For more green accommodation ideas go to Ⓦ www.godowales.com

Marine Wildlife Centre

Ⓦ www.cbmwc.org, see p.59

The Marine Wildlife Centre at New Quay in West Wales monitors the local dolphin population along the Ceredigion Coast. It is closely involved with marine environmental studies and ongoing protection of the dolphins' habitat.

Pembrokeshire Coastal Bus Services

Ⓦ www.pcnpa.org.uk

In 2000, five new bus services were introduced in the National Park, to provide coastal access for residents and visitors – the Celtic Coaster, Coastal Cruiser, Poppit Rocket, Puffin Shuttle and Strumble Shuttle. The 'Hail and Ride' buses can be flagged down as they pass, and last year carried over 60,000 passengers. In the seven years since they were launched, 30,000 car journeys have been avoided in the National Park.

Snowdonia Green Key

Ⓦ www.snowdoniagreenkey.co.uk

"Green Key" is a joint scheme to promote and expand the use of public transport in and around Snowdonia, and thereby cut down on car emissions and traffic congestion in one of the most popular parts of Wales. A bus service called the 'Snowdon Sherpa' has been introduced throughout the park.

St Davids Eco-City project

Ⓦ www.eco-city.co.uk

St Davids is on the way to becoming the first carbon-neutral city in the world. Many initiatives are already under way, including creating an EcoTrail to link up specific sites that demonstrate examples of renewable energy technology and biodiversity, motivating both local residents and the half-million annual visitors to play their own role, supplying biodiesel for local motorists, providing insulation and low-energy light-bulbs to help local households reduce their energy usage and even exploring the feasibility of installing a tidal turbine that could provide St Davids with 100% renewable energy.

Accommodation

elow is a listing of Visit Wales graded hostel, bunkhouse and YHA accommodation. Also listed are university halls of residence; these are available from June to mid-September only. Note also that places marked with an asterisk (★) mainly accept group bookings only. For a full listing visit ⓦwww.godowales.com

Southeast Wales

Cardiff Backpacker Cardiff
ⓣ029/2034 5577, ⓦwww.cardiff
backpacker.com.
Cardiff University Cardiff ⓣ029/2087
5508, ⓦwww.cardiff.ac.uk/resid.
Cardiff YHA Cardiff ⓣ0870/770
5750, ⓦwww.yha.org.uk.
Cynon Valley Bunkhouse Hirwaun
ⓣ01403/264641, ⓦwww.cyat.org.
Gower Bunkhouse Swansea
ⓣ01792/401548, ⓦwww.yha.org.uk.
★Gwersyll yr Urdd Caerdydd Cardiff
ⓣ029/2063 5678, ⓦwww.urdd
.org/caerdydd.
Hardingsdown Bunkhouse Swansea
ⓣ01792/386222, ⓦwww
.bunkhousegower.co.uk.
Hobo Backpackers Tredegar

ⓣ01495/718422, ⓦwww
.hobo-backpackers.com.
Merlins Backpackers Ystradgynlais,
nr Swansea ⓣ01639/845670,
ⓦwww.backpackerwales.com.
Nos Da at the Riverbank Cardiff
ⓣ029/2037 8866, ⓦwww.nosda
.co.uk.
Parc Bryn Bach Bunkhouse Tredegar
ⓣ01495/711816, ⓦwww.blaenau-
gwent.gov.uk.
Port Eynon YHA Swansea ⓣ0870/
770 5998, ⓦwww.yha.org.uk.
Red Oak Creek Creigiau ⓣ02920/
892999, ⓦwww.totalteambuilding
.com.
Rhossili Bunkhouse Swansea
ⓣ01792/401548, ⓦwww.yha.org.uk.
Riverside Hotel Monmouth
ⓣ01600/715577, ⓦwww.yha.org.uk.

Rose Cottage Cymmer ☎01639/
851820, ⓦwww.brynteghouse.com.
Swansea Bunkhouse Swansea
☎01792/401548, ⓦwww.yha.org.uk.
University of Glamorgan Pontypridd
☎01443/482002, ⓦwww
.glamorganconferenceservices.co.uk.
University of Wales Newport
Newport ☎01633/432800, ⓦwww
.newport.ac.uk.
University of Wales Swansea
Swansea ☎01792/295665, ⓦwww
.swan.ac.uk/conferences.

Southwest Wales

Broad Haven YHA Haverfordwest
☎0870/770 5728, ⓦwww.yha.org.uk.
Cae Iago Riding Centre Llanwrda
☎01558/650303, ⓦwww.caeiago.
co.uk.
Caerhafod Lodge Nr St. Davids
☎01348/837859, ⓦwww.caerhafod
.co.uk.
*Court House St Davids ☎01437/
720811, ⓦwww.courthouse.org.uk.
Manorbier YHA near Tenby ☎0870/
770 5954, ⓦwww.yha.org.uk.
Marloes Sands YHA Haverfordwest
☎0870/770 5958, ⓦwww.yha.org.uk.
Morfa Bunkhouse Pendine ☎01994/
453588, ⓦwww.morfabay.com.
Newgale YMCA Haverfordwest
☎01437/720959, ⓦwww.yha.org.uk.
Newport YHA Newport ☎0870/770
6072, ⓦwww.yha.org.uk.
Pant yr Athro International Hostel
Llansteffan ☎01267/241014, ⓦwww
.backpackershostelwales.co.uk.

Pembrokeshire Activity Centre
Pembroke Dock ☎01646/622013,
ⓦwww.princes-trust.org.uk/pac.
Preseli Venture Adventure Lodge
Haverfordwest ☎01348/837709,
ⓦwww.preseliventure.co.uk.
Pwll Deri YHA Goodwick ☎0870/770
6004, ⓦwww.yha.org.uk.
Sealyham Activity Centre Haverfordwest ☎01348/840763, ⓦwww
.sealyham.com.
St Davids YHA St Davids ☎0870/770
6042, ⓦwww.yha.org.uk.
*Upper Neeston Lodges Herbrand-
ston ☎01646/690750, ⓦwww
.upper-neeston.co.uk.

Central Wales

Absolute Adventure – Rhongyr Isaf
Centre Pen-y-Cae ☎01639/730518,
ⓦwww.absoluteadventure.co.uk.
Beili Neuadd Bunkhouse Rhayader
☎01597/810211, ⓦwww
.midwalesfarmstay.co.uk.
Black Mountain Lodge Abergavenny
☎01873/890208, ⓦwww
.theoldpandyinn.co.uk.
Brecon YHA Brecon ☎0870/770
5718, ⓦwww.yha.org.uk.
*Cadarn Bunkhouse Brecon
☎01497/847351, ⓦwww
.tregoydriding.co.uk.
*Cantref Bunkhouse Brecon ☎01874/
665223, ⓦwww.cantref.com.
Capel-y-Ffin YHA near Abergavenny
☎0870/770 5748, ⓦwww.yha.org.uk.
The Castle Inn – Trekkers Barn near
Talgarth ☎01874/711353, ⓦwww

.thecastleinn.co.uk.

Cwm Uchaf Bunkhouse Crai ☎01874/636703, Ⓦwww .bunkhouse.f9.co.uk.

Danywenallt YHA Brecon ☎0870/770 6136, Ⓦwww.yha.org.uk.

Dulwich Field Centre Penycae ☎01639/730892, Ⓦfieldcentre .dulwich.org.uk.

Ffrydd House Knighton ☎01547/ 520374, Ⓦwww.border-holidays.co.uk.

*Glynmeddig Barn Brecon ☎01874/638949, Ⓦwww .glynmeddigbarn.co.uk.

Granary Bunkhouse Penderyn ☎01685/811789, Ⓦwww .thebunkbarn.com.

*Held Bunkhouse Brecon ☎01874/624646, Ⓦwww .heldbunkhouse.co.uk.

*Joe's Lodge Brecon ☎07969/ 447438, Ⓦwww.joeslodge.co.uk.

Little Brompton Farm Montgomery ☎01686/668371, Ⓦwww.yha.org.uk.

Llanddeusant YHA Llanddeusant ☎0870/770 5930, Ⓦwww.yha .org.uk.

Llangattock Mountain Bunkhouse Crickhowell ☎01873/812307, Ⓦwww.yha.org.uk.

Llwyn-y-Celyn YHA Brecon ☎0870/ 770 5936, Ⓦwww.yha.org.uk.

*Maes Y Fron Abercraf ☎01639/ 700388, Ⓦwww.callofthewild.co.uk.

Maesbryncoch Barn Builth Wells ☎01982/551116, Ⓦwww .maesbryncochbarn.co.uk.

The Meeting House Penybont ☎01597/ 851951, Ⓦwww.thomas-shop.co.uk.

Middle Ninfa Farm Abergavenny ☎01873/854662, Ⓦwww .middleninfa.co.uk.

*Mount Severn Activity Centre Llanidloes ☎01686/412344, Ⓦwww.mountsevern.co.uk.

Mulberry House Abergavenny ☎01873/855959, Ⓦwww .yha.org.uk.

*Penstar Bunkhouse Brecon ☎01874/622702, Ⓦwww.penstar bunkhouseandcottage.co.uk.

*Perth-y-Pia Outdoor Centre Crick-howell ☎01873/810050, Ⓦwww .perth-y-pia.co.uk.

*Red Ridge Centre Welshpool ☎01938/ 810821, Ⓦwww.redridgecentre.co.uk.

Severn Farm B&B Welshpool ☎01938/555999, Ⓦwww.yha.org.uk.

Smithy's Bunkhouse Abergavenny ☎01873/853432, Ⓦwww .smithysbunkhouse.f9.co.uk.

Star Bunkhouse Brecon ☎01874/730080, Ⓦwww .starbunkhouse.com.

Trericket Mill Bunkhouse Builth Wells ☎01982/560312, Ⓦwww .trericket.co.uk.

Wain House Bunkhouse Llanthony ☎01873/890359, Ⓦwww.llanthony .co.uk.

Wern Watkin Bunkhouse Crickhowell ☎01873/812307, Ⓦwww .wernwatkin.co.uk.

White Hart Inn Talybont-on-Usk ☎01874/676227.

*Ynysmarchog Farm Bunkhouse Trecastle ☎01874/638000, Ⓦwww .bunkhousewales.com.

The Cambrian Coast

Borth YHA Borth ☏0870/770 5708,
⊛www.yha.org.uk.
Braich Goch Bunkhouse
Machynlleth ☏01654/761229,
⊛www.braichgoch.co.uk.
Bwlchcoediog Bunkhouse Machynlleth ☏01650/531329, ⊛www
.bwlchcoediog-bunkhouse.com.
*Canolfan Corris Hostel Machynlleth
☏01654/761686, ⊛www
.corrishostel.co.uk.
Dolgoch YHA Tregaron ☏0870/770
5976, ⊛www.yha.org.uk.
Fron Ifor Cardigan ☏01239/811565,
⊛www.tresaith.net.
Gwersyll Yr Udd Llangrannog
Llangrannog ☏01239/654473,
⊛www.urdd.org/llangrannog.
Kings YHA Dolgellau ☏0870/770
5900, ⊛www.yha.org.uk.
*Lodge at Llain Activity Centre
Llanarth ☏01545/580127, ⊛www
.llain.com.
*Longbarn Llandysul
☏01559/363200, ⊛www
.thelongbarn.co.uk.
Maes-y-Mor Hostel Aberystwyth
☏01970/639270, ⊛www.maesymor
.co.uk.
Marine Hotel Aberystwyth
☏01970/612444, ⊛www.marine
hotelaberystwyth.co.uk.
Plas Dolau Aberystwyth
☏01970/617834, ⊛www.dolau
-holidays.co.uk.
Poppit Sands Cardigan ☏0870/770
5996, ⊛www.yha.org.uk.

Reditreks Bunkhouse Machynlleth
☏01654/702184, ⊛www.reditreks
.com.
Tipiwest Cardigan ☏07813/672336,
⊛www.tipiwest.co.uk.
Tyncornel YHA Tregaron ☏0870/770
6113, ⊛www.yha.org.uk.
University of Wales Aberystwyth
Aberystwyth ☏01970/621960,
⊛www.aber.ac.uk/visitors.

Snowdonia and the Llŷn

Bala Backpackers Bala
☏01678/521700, ⊛www.bala
-backpackers.co.uk.
Bala Bunkhouse Bala ☏01678/
520738, ⊛www.balabunkhouse
.co.uk.
Betws-y-Coed YHA Betws-y-Coed
☏01690/710796, ⊛www.yha.org.uk.
Bobs Bunkhouse Caernarfon
☏0770/2233111, ⊛www
.bobsbunkhouse.co.uk.
Boulder Adventures Llanberis
☏01286/870556, ⊛www
.boulderadventures.co.uk.
Bryn Gwynant YHA Caernarfon
☏0870/770 5732, ⊛www.yha
.org.uk.
Capel Curig YHA Betws-y-Coed
☏0870/770 5746, ⊛www.yha.
org.uk
*Cornerstone Quest Bala ☏0121/
643 1984, ⊛www.cornerstone
.quest.co.uk.
The Eagles Betws-y-Coed
☏01690/760177, ⊛www
.eaglespenmachno.co.uk.

*Glan Dwr Mountain Lodge Capel Curig ☎01590/688011, 🌐www.hutaccomm.com.

Idwal Cottage YHA Bangor ☎0870/770 5874, 🌐www.yha.org.uk.

Llanberis YHA Llanberis ☎0870/770 5928, 🌐www.yha.org.uk.

Llys Ednowain Hostel Trawsfynydd ☎01766/770324, 🌐www.llysednowain.co.uk.

The Lodge Penmachno ☎01690/760181, 🌐www.tyred-out.com.

Ozanam Centre Llanllyfni ☎01286/881568, 🌐www.ozanamcentre.org.

Pentre Bach Camping Barn Caernarfon ☎01286/650643, 🌐www.bachventures.co.uk.

Pen-y-Pass YHA Caernarfon ☎0870/770 5990, 🌐www.yha.org.uk.

Snowdon Lodge Tremadog ☎0870/770 6038, 🌐www.snowdonlodge.co.uk.

Snowdon Ranger YHA Caernarfon ☎01766/515 354, 🌐www.yha.org.uk.

Woodlands Outdoor Centre Betws-y-Coed ☎0870/787 3326, 🌐www.woodlandscentre.co.uk.

Yr Helfa Llanberis ☎07900/087692, 🌐www.snowdonbunkhouse.co.uk.

The North Coast and Borderlands

Anglesey Outdoors Holyhead ☎01407/769351, 🌐www.yha.org.uk.

Bangor YHA Bangor ☎0870/770 5686, 🌐www.yha.org.uk.

Caban Cysgu Bethesda ☎01248/605573, 🌐www.cabancysgu-gerlan.co.uk.

Conwy YHA Conwy ☎0870/770 5774, 🌐www.yha.org.uk.

Ffynnon Wen YHA Conwy ☎01490/420349, 🌐www.yha.org.uk.

Fron Haul Guesthouse Bodfari ☎01745/710301, 🌐www.yha.org.uk.

The Goat Inn Corwen ☎01490/413465, 🌐www.activitypubs.co.uk.

Lake House Holidays Anglesey ☎01248/853024, 🌐www.lakehouseholidays.com.

Llandudno Hostel Llandudno ☎01492/877430, 🌐www.llandudnohostel.co.uk.

Llangollen YHA Llangollen ☎0870/770 5932, 🌐www.yha.org.uk.

*Outdoor Alternative Holyhead ☎01407/860469, 🌐www.outdooralternative.org.

Rowen YHA Conwy ☎0870/770 6012, 🌐www.yha.org.uk.

St Deiniol's Library Hawarden ☎01244/532350, 🌐www.st-deiniols.org.

Tyddyn Bychan Bunkhouse Corwen ☎01490/420680, 🌐www.tyddynbychan.co.uk.

University of Wales Bangor Bangor ☎01248/388399, 🌐www.welcomebangor.co.uk.

Wynnstay Arms Llangollen ☎01978/860710, 🌐www.wynnstay-arms.co.uk.

Annual events

Visit Wales maintains up-to-date listings of many festivals and events on its websites, ⓦwww.godowales.com and ⓦwww.visitwales.com.

January

1st Mari Llwyd, Llangynwyd, near Maesteg. Most authentic survivor of the ancient Welsh custom of parading a horse's skull through the village streets.

February & March

All month Six Nations rugby championship ⓦwww.millenniumstadium .com. Last won by Wales in 2005.

March

1st St Davids Day. Celebrations all over Wales.

May

Late May The Full Ponty, Pontypridd ⓦwww.thefullponty.com. Live music and great bands at Pontypridd's Ynysangharad Park.
Late May to early June Hay Festival

of Literature ⓦwww.hayfestival.co.uk. Britain's "town of books" is the ideal setting for this international literary festival.
Late May to early June Urdd National Eisteddfod ⓦwww.urdd.org. Vast and enjoyable youth eisteddfod – the largest youth festival in Europe – which alternates between North and South Wales.

June

Mid-June Man versus Horse Marathon, Llanwrtyd Wells ⓦllanwrtyd -wells.powys.org.uk. A 22-mile race between runners, cyclists and horses – a runner won for the first time in 2004.

July

July/August Cardiff Summer Festival ⓦwww.cardiff-festival.com. This international summer festival features the best in street theatre, live music, children's entertainment, and Celtic food and drink, culminating in "The Big Weekend", the UK's largest free open-air festival.

Early July Llangollen International Musical Eisteddfod ⓦ www.international-eisteddfod.co.uk. Over twelve thousand participants from all over the world, including choirs, dancers, folk singers, groups and instrumentalists.

Mid–July Sesiwn Fawr (Big Session), Dolgellau ⓦ www.sesiwnfawr.co.uk. Musicians and festival-goers descend on Dolgellau for a superb weekend of Celtic bands, rock, pop — and beer.

Mid–July Wakestock, Abersoch ⓦ www.wakestock.co.uk. Europe's largest wakeboard festival. Two days of cutting-edge music and wakeboarding, an exciting mix of snowboarding, surfing and skateboarding, out on the Llŷn Peninsula.

Mid–Late July Royal Welsh Show, Builth Wells ⓦ www.rwas.co.uk. Wales' main annual agricultural showpiece.

Late July The Big Cheese, Caerphilly ⓦ www.caerphilly.gov.uk/bigcheese. A huge family-oriented festival with street entertainers, music, dance, a traditional funfair, folk dancing, falconry, fire eating and, of course, cheese.

August

Early August National Eisteddfod of Wales ⓦ www.eisteddfod.org.uk. Wales's biggest single annual event: fun, very impressive and worth seeing if only for the overblown pageantry. Bardic competitions, readings, theatre, TV, debates and copious help for the Welsh-language learner.

Mid–August Brecon Jazz Festival, Powys ⓦ www.breconjazz.co.uk. Widely regarded as one of the best in Britain.

Mid–August The Green Man Festival ⓦ www.thegreenmanfestival.co.uk. An alternative 3 day folk festival in the Brecon Beacons.

Late August Llandrindod Wells Victorian Festival, Powys ⓦ www .vicfest.co.uk. A week of family fun, street entertainment and Victorian costumes rounded off with a fireworks display and torchlit procession.

Late August Faenol Festival, near Bangor ⓦ www.brynfest.com. Originated by opera megastar Bryn Terfel, the three-day event now encompasses all kinds of music.

Late August Big Balloon Festival, Blackwood ⓦ www.caerphilly.gov.uk/bigballoon. A free festival that includes a spectacular mass balloon launch, street entertainers, live music, funfair and a fireworks display.

Last Monday World Bog Snorkelling Championships, Llanwrtyd Wells ⓦ llanwrtyd-wells.powys.org.uk. Competitors travel from all over the world to snorkel the length of a peaty murky trench in a Mid-Wales bog. Incorporates a mountain-bike bog-leaping contest.

September

First Saturday Cardiff Mardi Gras
ⓦ www.cardiffmardigras.co.uk. This
lesbian and gay festival consists of
live acts, dance tents and stalls in the
grounds of the capital's castle.

**Mid-September Abergavenny
Food Festival** ⓦ www
.abergavennyfoodfestival.com. A high-
profile festival celebrating local and
regional food and drink which attracts
foodies from all over the UK.

Late September Elvis Festival, Porthcawl ⓦ www.elvies.co.uk. The biggest
Elvis festival in Europe, attracting trib-
ute acts from all over the world.

November–December

**Mid November–early January Win-
ter Wonderland**, Cardiff ⓦ www
.cardiffswinterwonderland.com. Outdoor ice-skating and entertainment on
Cardiff's City Hall lawn.

**Early November Dylan Thomas Fes-
tival**, Swansea ⓦ www.dylanthomas
festival.com. Talks, performances,
exhibitions, readings and music with
a DT theme.

**Mid November Mid-Wales Beer
Festival**, Llanwrtyd Wells ⓦ llanwrtyd
-wells.powys.org.uk. Highly social
festival with all sorts of entertainment
around local hostelries. The largest
festival of its kind in Wales, if not the
UK, lasting for a full ten days, with over
sixty different ales to choose from.

**End November–early December
Wales Rally GB** ⓦ www
.walesrallygb.com. Four days of world-
class competitive driving over 1300km
of mountainous terrain and rugged
forest tracks throughout Mid-, South
and West Wales.